# Is it in the BIBLE?

# Is it in the BIBLE?

DIALOGUING WITH FRIENDS

Rev. Jude O. Mbukanma, O.P.

Nihil Obstat
Colum Daley, O.P.
January 5, 1978

Imprimatur
+ **Anthony Olubunmi Okogie, D. D.**
Archbishop of Lagos
January 5th, 1978

First published by the Dominican
Publication, March, 1978
Second Edition, July, 1978
Third Edition, October, 1980
Reprinted 1982, 1983, 1984
Fourth Edition, May, 1987
Fifth Edition, August, 1993
Sixth Edition, August, 1994

Published by M.E.T. Ltd.
P. O. Box 14, Clifton, Virginia, 22024

ISBN: 0-949154-12-1

# PREFACE

This book, "Is it in the Bible" has been written to answer various questions which people ask about some Catholic beliefs. The answers are given in simple language so that believers who are not trained theologians will be able to understand them and to explain their beliefs to others.

Because some people insist that every Catholic belief and practice must have its authority from the Bible, the booklet has considered the questions from the Biblical point of view. Therefore, while reading it, it is very important to listen to the teachings of the Church and to be guided by them in trying to understand what the Bible is teaching.

The Church existed before the Bible as we have it today. After His resurrection, Jesus told His disciples, "Go, therefore make disciples of all nations; baptize them in the name of the Father and of the Son and of the Holy Spirit, and teach them to observe all the commands I gave you. And know that I am with you always; yes, to the end of time" (Mt. 28:19-20). The disciples, therefore, began to tell people about Jesus, they began to preach and to make disciples and to baptize. They did not immediately sit down to write the Gospels and Epistles. Therefore, the Church existed for many years before the Bible as we have it today.

According to Biblical Scholars, the first part of the New Testament to be written was St. Paul's first letter to the Thessalonians which he wrote around the year 51 AD, which was about 18 years after the death of Jesus. When the early members of the Church began to write, they did not write down everything they were preaching, nor did they write down everything that Jesus said and did. For St. John's Gospel tells us, "But there are also many other things which Jesus did; were everyone of them to be written, I suppose that the world itself could not contain the books that would be written" (Jn. 21:25). The Church, under the inspiration of the Holy Spirit, continues to teach today what Jesus taught even though it was not all written down.

Shortly before His death, Jesus said to his disciples, "I have yet many things to say to you, but you cannot bear them now. When the Spirit of truth comes, he will guide you into all the truth; for he will not speak on his own authority, but whatever he hears he will speak, and he will declare to you the things that are to come" (Jn. 16:12-13).

The Spirit continues to guide the Church into the truth. Jesus, through his Spirit, continues to speak to us today through the Church. Therefore, as we read the Bible, we should listen to Jesus speaking to us not only in the words of the Bible but also through the Church. If our understanding of the Bible is different from that of the Church, then we should know that our own interpretation is incorrect, and we should prayerfully re-read the Bible and listen to the Lord again. May the Lord Jesus open our mind and our heart so that we might listen to the Word of God and that we might live in His Spirit to the honour and glory of God the Father.

E. H. Riley, O.P.
September 8, 1983
Feast of the Birth of Mary

# FOREWORD
## TO SECOND EDITION

Before this book was first published, I wrote to the Catholic Archbishop of Lagos, Rt. Rev. A.O. Okogie, for an imprimatur. In that letter to His Grace, I said this: *"Some people outside our faith over and over again attack our doctrines and Catholic practices; and some young Catholics have left the Church to join other Christian organisations because we do not seem to answer some of their questions on Catholic doctrines. The young ones have an increasing love for the word of God and would like to see our faith flowing from the authority of the sacred word and articulated tradition. So, my efforts in that small book is this: to explain the Catholic beliefs and practices from the angle of the sacred word; in other words, I wish to show that what we do in the Catholic Church is what the Bible teaches and what our holy tradition accepts as revealed."* This remains my aim in this second edition.

I have now come to know, judging from the rush for the first publication of this book, that a good number of the Nigerian Catholics are interested in knowing and defending their faith. I hope that this second edition which has few additional exciting topics, will meet the needs of all those Catholics who wish to share their faith with other people.

I wish to express my deepest gratitude to Bro. Stephen Lucas, O.P., who lovingly did the great job of having this book published. I also wish to express my hearty thanks to the following:

The Very Rev. Ambrose Windbacher, O.P., my Vicar Provincial, who graciously agreed to contribute some articles to this second edition; The Superior of St. Dominic's House, Yaba, Fr. Column Daley, O.P., and the rest of my brothers in St. Dominic, for their encouragements.

JUDE O. MBUKANMA, O.P.

*This book is
dedicated to the
Holy Spirit of Truth,
the great teacher
of those who believe
in the
Lord Jesus Christ.*

# THE TEACHING OF THE BIBLE ON DIALOGUE

## What is the right attitude in dialoguing with friends?

(Ecclesiasticus 5:10-13; 1 Pet. 3:15).

The sub-title of this book is "Dialoguing with Friends". Dialogue is the most difficult thing to do; disagreement always arises precisely because no two persons can see the same issue exactly in the same way. Why two persons cannot see truth exactly in the same way is because of the differences in their frame of mind, education, interest, etc. That people disagree on the teachings of the Bible is basically due to the reasons I have given here. But we must all continue to read the Bible. To understand the truth therein, we must read it on our bended knees. We should search through the Scriptures to know the Lord better and to be able to uphold the truth. We read in the Bible that this was the practice of the early Church:

"They listened to the message with great earnestness, and every day they studied the Scriptures to see if what Paul said was true" (Acts 17:11).

In dialoguing with friends on the Catholic teaching, we should be gentle and say only what we know, and then be silent. "There are times when silence is better than debate, and is a truer comment than any which debate could arrive at, whether proof or disproof" (Geoffrey Ashe, Miracles, p. 121).

We do not have the power to understand everything the Bible teaches. The Catholic Church, happily enough, is here to guide us. It is important to know that we are not obliged to answer every question about the mysteries of faith which somebody might ask us. It is necessary to discern the motive of the questioner. We should learn from Jesus. He dialogued with people but there were times He kept quiet when He was asked questions. Consider His reactions to the following questions:

(i) "On what authority are you doing all these things ..." Jesus' answer was: "... neither will I tell you" (Mk. 11:28, 33). According to Luke, when Herod questioned Him during His trial, not even a word of defence came from His lips (Lk. 23:9; Is. 50:5-7).

(ii) The teachers of the law and the Pharisees brought in a woman to Him. "Teacher", they said to him, "this woman has been caught in the act of adultery. In the law, Moses ordered such a woman to be stoned. What do you have to say about the case?" (Jn. 8:4-5). They wanted to trap Jesus but Jesus maintained silence. Then he wrote on the ground. This was not an answer to the question He was asked. He however, said to the people: "Let the man among you who has no sin be the first to cast a stone at her" (Jn. 8:7).

This was not an answer to their question. The action of Jesus was equal to silence. Why did Jesus refuse to give an answer? The questioners were not asking to know the truth and so it would have been pointless if Jesus had expounded the true doctrine to them. An example comes to mind: When Pilate asked Jesus: "What is truth?" (Jn. 18:38), He, Pilate did not wait to have an answer, for he was not looking for an answer. We must learn to know when to speak and when to be silent.

Sometimes, someone might come to you and ask: "Is devotion to the Blessed Virgin of Nazareth in the Bible?" If you have the feeling that he is not really interested in knowing the truth, you will do well not to talk to him on the matter. Where there is no pure motive, no teaching will make sense to a questioner.

In dialogue, if you don't know the answer to a question, don't say anything that will confuse the issue. On the whole, the teaching of the Bible on dialogue is:

"Stand firmly by what you know and be consistent in what you say. Be quick to listen, but take time over your answer. Answer a man if you know what to say but if not, hold your tongue. Honour or shame can come through speaking and a man's tongue may be his downfall" (Ecclesiasticus 5:10-13).

We should not get our ideas mixed up in a dialogue. A good number of people do not know how to stick to a subject; the result is that you get confused in the process of the dialogue. Somebody came to me one day and asked me:

"Father, do you believe in the power of the saints to pray for you?" "Do you believe in the infallibility of the Pope?" The questions were too many, so I decided to discuss only one of them with her at that meeting.

But in the process of discussion, she kept on bringing in the other question as if it was logically connected with the one we were discussing. I told her to keep to one topic at a time. This is the right attitude in dialogue. Never dabble into various issues at the same time.

May the Holy Spirit take complete control of your whole being as you bear witness to the truth.

Jude O. Mbukanma, O.P.
December 8, 1983.
Feast of the Immaculate Conception.

# INTRODUCTION

"Always be prepared to make a defence to anyone who calls you to account for the hope that is in you, yet do it with gentleness and reverence" (1 Peter 3:15).

In the few pages of this booklet, I shall attempt an explanation of those beliefs and practices of the Catholic Church which are very often questioned by some people; and where possible, I shall support my brief explanation with relevant passages from the Holy Scripture. The explanations are brief but you have a good number of references to make in the Scripture in case you are engaged in talking to those who want to know what you do in your Church.

In the light of my own experience, most of our Catholics do not read the Scriptures enough to be able to explain the Catholic doctrines whenever they are questioned. I know this to have been true when I was an active Legionary. So, the impression we give to the world is that some of our beliefs and practices have no foundation in the Bible.

The Catholic doctrines are based on the Holy Scripture and on the Apostolic Traditions. They are not therefore, human ideas formulated to suit her members' religious emotions. So do not be afraid. TAKE UP YOUR BIBLE AND STUDY.

Besides the need to instruct people and correct errors (2 Timothy 3:16), the Holy Scripture should be consulted more often because it is the basis of Christian Spirituality. The words of the Scripture are life and they lead to salvation. We should all try to dive deep into this book of life for the treasures buried in it.

The explanations here are my own personal work and all criticisms against any shortcomings therein should be placed squarely on my shoulders.

Rev. Jude O. Mbukanma, O.P.
Dominican Community, Ibadan.
19th November, 1975

# CONTENTS

# QUESTIONS

## Q. 1 (a) Is Jesus Christ God?
## (b) Are there three persons in one God?

If Jesus is God and the Holy Spirit is God, does that mean that there are three Gods? No. There is only one God. The existence of the Three Persons in One God is a mystery; that is, something which is true but which we could never have known were it not revealed to us by God Himself. This mystery remains so because man's knowledge of God in the present life is purely intellectual, weak, and hazy.

God became man in the person of Jesus Christ. But when Jesus Christ was on earth, he did not go about shouting that he is God. He wanted people to know this without being told so. He wanted his life to speak for him. Listen to what he told Philip, one of his disciples. *"Have I been with you so long, and yet you do not know me, Philip? He who has seen me has seen the Father: how can you say* "show us the Father" ... *Believe me that I am in the Father and the Father in me; or else believe me for the sake of the works themselves"* (John 14:9-11).

If Jesus had gone around telling people: *"I am Yahweh",* would he have found it easy to mix up with the people? Would his eating and drinking with the people not be a big scandal; and in fact, a denial of his claim that he is God? Does God eat and drink? One thing seems clear: If Jesus had told the Jews right from his boyhood that he is God, the kind of claim that he made during his trial (Matt. 26:64), he would probably have been pursued and killed earlier than he was.

It is difficult to understand how Jesus can be both God and man. Though we cannot understand it, it remains true that Jesus is God. I will now give you series of scriptural quotations in support of this truth:

(1) In the prophecy of Isaiah, we see the nature of Christ fore-told. *"... Wonder-counsellor, Mighty-God, Eternal-Father, Prince of Peace"* (Isaiah 9:1-7).

(2) *"In the beginning was the Word, the Word was with God, and the Word was God ... And the Word became flesh and dwelt among us ..."* (John 1:1 and 14).

(3) *"To have seen me is to have seen the Father".* (John 14:8-11).

(4) *"... the Father is in me and I am in the Father"* (John 10:38).

(5) *"Go therefore, make disciples of all the nations; baptize them in the name of the Father, and of the Son and of the Holy Spirit"* (Matt. 28:19).

1

The above quotations show the divinity of Jesus Christ. Other scriptural evidences about the Trinity are cited below:

(6) *"I shall ask the Father and He will give you another Advocate to be with you forever, that Spirit of truth"* (John 14:16).

Note the use of the word Advocate here. An advocate is a person who pleads for another. Some people think that the Holy Spirit is a kind of impersonal force emanating from God and moving people to do things. No. The Bible tells us that the Holy Spirit is a distinct personality that proceeds from God. Jesus said:

(7) *"These things I have spoken to you, while I am still with you but the Counsellor, the Holy Spirit, whom that Father will send in my name, he will teach you all things and bring to your remembrance all that I have said to you"* (John 14:25-26).

Mark the words used here. The Holy Spirit is a counsellor and a teacher.

Some Bibles use the word 'Paraclete' for the Holy Spirit. The meaning is the same. *"The word 'paraclete' can be translated many different ways: advocate, counsellor, guide, intercessor, protector, support. A paraclete was the person who stood by the defendant in a trial in a courtroom. He was on the defendant's side and gave him all the help and advice which the defendant needed. Jesus was saying that just as he had been a paraclete, an advocate, for his disciples, so the Holy Spirit would be a new paraclete".* Let us listen to what St. Paul has to say about Jesus.

(8) His state was divine yet he did not cling to his equality with God (Phil. 2:6).

(9) For in him all the fullness of God was pleased to dwell (Col. 1:19; 2:9).

Further references: 1 Tim. 1:17; Tit. 2:13.

It is possible to try to explain this big mystery of the trinity without making reference to the Holy Scripture. It is understood that St. Patrick did try to use a simple leaf to illustrate it. This is splendid. However, no evidence is more acceptable and authentic than that of the Scripture on the subject.

Jesus is God. Only faith can accept this truth. If we are truly Christians, we should accept this mystery on the authority of Jesus. It is not a matter for mathematical proof.

# Q. 2 Do we worship images?

Some people think that it is wrong to use holy pictures, medals, crucifixes, rosaries, and other sacramentals in our religious devotions. According to these people, the Bible does not permit the use of images for worship; for to use them would amount to the worship of idols. Certainly, only God should be adored or worshipped. Adoration belongs to God alone. This is the Catholic teaching. But it is wrong to say that the Bible does not permit the making and the use of images as an aid for religious devotion. We shall see what the Scripture says about this.

Take up a picture or something which reminds you of someone you love and then you will realize the truth in the statement of Confuscius that *"a picture is worth a thousand words"*.

The Catholic Church teaches that *"images must not be prayed to because they can neither hear, see, nor help us"*. In other words, the images have no life.

Why then do we have images in the Church? They are used in the Church to help Christians to meditate on the lives of our Lord and the saints which they represent. Furthermore, images help to arouse a feeling of religious devotion and develop a spirit of contemplation.

The Scripture certainly condemns the worship of images. The prophets called such an offence prostitution; that is, an act of infidelity to the love God has for man. But there is however, evidence in the Bible that God did allow the making of images for religious devotion. I will now cite below several passages in the Bible to support this fact:

(1) *Yahweh said to Moses: "Make a fiery serpent and put it on a standard. If anyone is bitten and looks at it, he shall be healed".* (Num. 21:8-9).

This is not to say that the image of a fiery serpent healed the people who were bitten. It was God who healed them but He effected the healing through the use of the fiery serpent. Today, we do not look on the fiery serpent for our salvation. We have something better: The Cross of Jesus – Col. 1:20; 2:14; John 12:32.

(2) Yahweh said: *"... You are to make two golden cherubs; you are to make them of beaten gold ... The cherubs are to have their wings spread. There I shall come to meet you".* (Ex. 25:17-22).

A cherub is an angel. Here, Yahweh (God) asked Moses to fashion two images of Angels-Cherubs. These images were to be placed on the Ark. Yahweh concluded that He would meet Moses there.

In Exodus 27:20, we see also that Yahweh asked Moses to put up a light that would burn perpetually before the Ark of Testimony. This Ark was a sign of God's promise to His people and His presence among them. In order to make this presence felt and understood in some way, Yahweh asked the people to build images of two of His Angels and place them on the Ark; and also to put up a light before the Ark perpetually.

David danced before the Ark, feeling confident that God was 'present' therein. God did not condemn him. Read 2 Sam. 6:13-14 and 21. In Revelation 8:2-5, we are told that incense was offered before God but God was not angry. In Genesis 9:12-17, we see God making use of a sign: *"Here is the sign of the covenant I make between myself and you ... I set my BOW in the clouds ..."*

Having regard to all these evidences from the Sacred Scripture, we can safely conclude that God does not condemn the making of images but He condemns the worship of them. We need the things of this world to think about things beyond our knowledge. There is nothing wrong in the use of blessed medals, holy pictures, crucifixes, rosaries, if these can help us to lift our minds to God. God can make use of any of these in showing us His love and mercy. The Scripture bears witness to this:

*"And God did extraordinary miracles by the hands of Paul, so that handkerchiefs or aprons were carried away from his body to the sick, and diseases left them and the evil spirits came out of them"* (Acts 19:11-12).

The crucifix is not the object of our thought when we look at it. It isn't the crucifix that the Christians adore; it is Jesus Christ, whose image is engraved on the wood, that is adored. The crucifix therefore recalls to mind the passion of Jesus and the goodness of God. The Christian must lift his mind beyond the cross to Jesus who has come to save him and the world.

When we see the Armed Forces stand at attention to salute a country's flag, we know that they are paying respect to the country the flag represents, and not that they are giving a salute to a lifeless object, the flag. The wedding ring symbolises marriage and to wear it does not mean that one is married to the ring. We certainly have to go beyond the images to the things they represent. When David danced before the Ark (2 Sam. 6:13-14 and 21), his mind certainly went beyond the wooden box.

# Q. 3 (a) How many people will go to heaven?

The Sacred Scripture does not tell us the number of those who will go to heaven. The Sacred Scripture has however specified the KIND of people that will see God when they die.

The teaching of the Holy Scripture is that anybody who lives a good life will go to heaven when he dies. The Bible says:
(1) *"But the souls of the virtuous are in the hands of God, no torment shall ever touch them. In the eyes of the unwise, they did appear to die ... they are in peace"* (Wisdom 3:1-3).

4

(2) *"... all we know is, that when it is revealed, we shall be like him, because we shall see him as he really is"* (1 John 3:2).

(3) *"And men will come from east and west, and north and south, and sit at table in the kingdom of God"* (Luke 13:29).

(4) "Happy are the pure in heart: They shall see God" "... Your reward is in heaven" (Matt. 5:8 and 12).

(5) *"... They will see him face to face"* (Rev. 22:3-5).

(6) *"... Who will enter the kingdom of heaven but the person who does the will of my Father in heaven".* (Matt. 7:21). Some people say that 144,000 people will inherit heaven. This is absurd – Rev. 7:4. Where will the rest of millions of other virtuous mankind go? To hell? If 144,000 are sealed, who are the crowds referred to in verse nine in this seventh chapter? Rev. 7:9 says: *"after this I looked, and behold a great multitude which no man could number".* "The crowds are the new Israel of God" (Gal. 6:16). *"They have arrived at that blessed state because they have passed through Great tribulation viz: the special suffering experienced by every follower of Jesus. ("He who does not take up his cross and follow me is not worthy of me"* (Matt. 10:38 – The book of the Apocalypse by William G. Heidt, O.S.B.).

(7) *"The virtuous will shine like the sun in the Kingdom of their Father"* (Matt. 13:43).

(8) *"Father, I want those you have given me to be with me where I am, so that they may always see the glory you have given me ..."* (John. 17:24).

# Q. 3 (b) Are we invited to heaven?

**The Bible says that we are invited to heaven**

(9) *"Take for your heritage the Kingdom prepared for you"* (Matt. 25:34).

(10) *"... There is a house built by God for us, an everlasting home not made by human hands, in the heavens"* (2 Cor. 5:1).

(11) *"Through him, both of us have in the one spirit our way to come to the Father".* (Eph. 2:18). *Believers will see Christ in his glory on the last day.* (2 Thess. 1:7 and 10).

(12) *"... We will be taken up in the clouds, together with them, to meet the Lord in the air, so we shall stay with the Lord forever",* (1 Thess. 4:17).

(13) *Christians are called through the good news to* "share the glory of our Lord Jesus Christ" (2 Thess. 2:14, Ref: Heb. 4:9; Rev. 14:13).

(14) *"Christ died to lead us to God ..."* (1 Pet. 3:18).

(15) *"... They will see Him face to face ...* (Rev. 22:4).

(16) *"... You see this city? here God lives among men. He will make His home among them ..."* Rev. 21:3 Refs. John 12:32; 1 Cor. 2:9; 1 John 3:2; Matt. 25:31-46.


## Q. 4 Can a man be called holy or saint?

God is holy. He is not selfish. Because of this simple fact, He has given mankind the means to be holy too. It is wrong to say that the word 'holy' or 'saint' should only apply to God. The Bible says that we are called to be holy. Read through the following passages from the Holy Scripture.

(1) *"Be holy, for I, Yahweh your God, am holy"* (Lev. 19:2).

(2) *"... You have been sanctified and have become holy because I am holy ..."* (Lev. 11:44 and 45).

(3) *"He raised up Aaron, a holy man like Moses, his brother of the tribe of Levi".* (Ecclesiasticus 45:6).

(4) *"You must therefore be perfect just as your heavenly Father is perfect"* (Matt. 5:48).

(5) *"... Be holy yourselves ..."* (1 Pet. 1:15-16).

(6) *"... Be Saintly and religious ..."* (1 Tim. 6:11).

(7) *"... To live a holy life is to be holy just as he is holy"* (1 John 3:7-8).

Jesus has called us to share his holiness. Holiness is having the life of Jesus and working in his spirit. He said:
"I came that they may have life, and have it abundantly". (John 10:10). *Jesus is the bread of life that came down from heaven. He who eats his flesh and drinks his blood will live in Jesus and he Jesus will live in the person* (John 6:41 & 56). *Jesus is the source of our holiness* (1 Cor. 1:30). *He wants us to be holy just as our heavenly Father is holy* (Matt. 5:48).

Further references: Matt. 27:52; 2 Cor. 13:12; Romans 15:25; Heb. 3:1; Eph. 1:4-5; Col. 1:22; 1 Thess 4:3; Eph. 5: 3-4; 1 Cor. 16:1; 2 Pet. 1:3. If you read through these passages, you will see where the words 'holy or saint' is used for mortal men or where we are called to be holy. So having regard to the evidence of the Holy Scripture, men can certainly be holy or Saints or addressed as such.


## Q. 5 (a) Has God any house?

God is a spirit (John 4:24) and so lives in all places. There are those who tell us that God could not live in a house made with human hands. I disagree. If God is a spirit and He lives everywhere, then He lives also in the house dedicated to His honour and glory; that is, a house set aside in which a community of believers worships Him.

Before we go to the Scripture, it is worthwhile to point out certain important facts: (1) It is the nature of man to live, meet and do things in common. This is the basic reason why people are attracted to community worship. (2) God, as a matter of fact, does not need a house because He cannot be confined to a place. Being everywhere, He can see, hear and communicate with His children wherever they are on earth. It is for the benefit of man that God sanctions places dedicated to His worship.

We will now refer to the Holy Scripture to hear what it has to say about places of worship:

(1) *"Build me a sanctuary so that I may dwell with them"* (Ex. 25:8).

(2) *"In every place in which I have my name remembered I shall come to you and bless you. If you make me an altar of stone, do not build it of dressed stone".* (Ex. 20:24-26).

(3) *"I will make them joyful in my house of prayer"* (Isaiah 56:7).

(4) *"My house shall be called a house of prayer"* (Matt. 21:13; Jer. 7:9-10).

Further references: Eph. 3:10; 1 Tim. 3:15; James 5:14; Acts 2:46, John 2:16-17. *"Happy are those who live in your house and praise you all day long"* (Psalm 84:4), 1 Cor. 4:17; 15:9; Acts 13:1; 9:31; 14:23; Romans 16:23. In the New Testament, the word 'Church' is used mostly to refer to those who believe in Jesus.

# Q. 5 (b) Who founded the Church?

Jesus Christ founded the Church which we now call the Catholic Church when he said:

*Blessed are you, Simon Bar-Jona!*
*... And I tell you, you are Peter,*
*and on this rock I will build my Church ..."*
(Matt. 16:17-18).

Because of the world-wide mission of the Church, it became known as the Catholic Church. The Church is in the world for the salvation of the human race. On account of this her universal mission, it is called Catholic Church. So, do not expect to find the word 'Catholic' in the Bible. You will only find the word 'Church' in the Bible. It is the Church that is *"the pillar and bulwark of the truth"* (1 Tim. 3:15) *through which* "the manifold wisdom of God may be made known" *(Eph. 3:10).*

Peter in the passage quoted above (Matt. 16:17-18) was made the first visible head of the Church. Since the time of Peter to the present day, the Church has had an unbroken chain of leadership. The head of the Catholic Church today, is therefore, on the direct link with the successive heads of the whole Church at different ages from the time of the first head, Peter. This is why we say that the Catholic Church was founded by Jesus Christ.

The Church calls the successor of Peter, the Pope. This is a name the Church has decided to give her head. He, like Peter, is the visible head of the Church. He has been given certain powers by Christ (Matt. 16:19). Jesus is the invisible head of the Church (Eph. 5:23; Col. 1:18).

# Q. 6 (a) Why do we venerate the saints and ask for their prayers?
### (See also Question 32)

The Catholic Church does not canonize any of her departed children because of their extraordinary life of miracles. The Church canonizes heroes of faith – those who have really loved and served their fellow men. Miracles are therefore, complementary demands for canonization.

Since Jesus Christ is the only mediator between God and man, why then do we ask the saints to pray for us? The Holy Scripture tells us why:

(1) The prayer of honest men is dear to Yahweh (Prov. 15:8).

(2) *"Yahweh stands far from the wicked, but He listens to the prayers of the virtuous* (Prov. 15:29). Read Job 42:8; James 5:16.

But how do we know that somebody is a saint and who has the right to proclaim a person a saint? The Church has the power to judge that a person has done well or that he has not lived a good life. Jesus told the apostles whose authority the Church shares:

(3) *"I will give you the keys of the kingdom of heaven, and whatever you bind on earth shall be bound in heaven, and whatever you loose on earth shall be loosed in heaven"* (Matt. 16:19).

If you say that this authority was given only the apostles, then the authority to preach the good news (see Matt. 28:19) ceases at the death of the apostles; and in fact, Paul would have been wrong too to judge and to teach that the Church has the power to judge. Listen to what the Bible says:

(4) *"I have pronounced judgment in the name of the Lord on the man who has done such a thing. Deliver this man to satan for the destruction of the flesh so that his spirit may be saved in the day of the Lord Jesus"* (1 Cor. 5:3-5).

(5) *"Is it not those inside the Church you are to judge?"* (1 Cor. 5:12).

We can trust the Church's judgment as to who is a saint because Jesus Christ has promised her that he will be with her to the end of the world (Matt. 28:20) and that he will give her the Holy Spirit of truth to lead her to the truth (John 14:25; 17:17). Paul also tells us that the Church of the living God, upholds the truth and keeps it safe (1 Timothy 3:15).

The reason however, why we ask the saints to pray for us, is simply because the Saints are closer to God than we are; they are, as the Scripture says, those:

(6) "... *who have come out of the great tribulation; they have washed their robes and made them white in the blood of the lamb. Therefore are they before the throne of God ..."* (Rev. 7:14-15).

They have been glorified.

The great tribulation they had gone through, is the normal suffering which every Christian has to undergo before entering into the kingdom of heaven (He who does not take up his cross and follow me, is not worthy of me" (Matt. 10:38).

We ask the prayers of our fellow men even though we know that we could pray directly to God (Heb. 13:18). We hear God in the Scripture saying:

(7) "... *Job, my servant, offers prayers for you. I will listen to him with favour ...* (Job 42:8-10).

*If we can pray for one another in this life, who can we not continue to do so after death?* (Eph. 6:18).

For the veneration of the saints, read an Old Testament practice in Ecclesiasticus 44:1; and also Chapters 45-50. Paul also says: imitate those who are good in the Church (Phil. 3:17); imitate the saints because they are good in the Church.

# Q. 6 (b) Mary in the Catholic Church
## (See also Questions 40 and 41)

Catholics love Mary because of the beautiful role she played in the work of man's salvation. It was she whom God chose to be the mother of Jesus, the God-man. Since Jesus is both God and man, Mary is therefore called to be the mother of God. The Church says: *"She is the favourite daughter of the Father and the temple of the Holy Spirit. Because of this gift of sublime grace she far surpasses all other creatures, both in heaven and on earth"* (Vat. 2).

In the Old Testament, the prophets pointed out her role in the work of salvation.

(1) The woman will crush the serpent's head (Gen. 3:15). The serpent that led man into sin. Take note: JB translates the text to read: "It will crush your head and you will strike its heels". (Gen. 3:15). JB says: "The Latin version has a feminine pronoun ('She' will crush ...) and since, in the

9

Messianic interpretation of our text, the Messiah and his Mother appear together, the pronoun has been taken to refer to Mary; this application has become current in the Church" (JB. p.19). The Good News Bible says "Her offspring will crush your head (Satan), and you will bite THEIR heel" (Gen 3:15).

(2) The Lord himself will give you a sign. It is this, the maiden is with child and will soon give birth to a son whom she will call Immanuel (Is. 7:14). The Greek version of the Bible reads *"the Virgin"* in place of *"Maiden"*. The Church sees in this prophecy a hidden reference to the birth of Christ.

The New Testament points out also Mary's holiness and role in the work of salvation. God has 'so highly favoured her (Luke 1:29).

(3) *"For behold, henceforth all generations will call me blessed"* (Luke 1:48).

The honour we give to Mary therefore, is the honour which the Bible says should be given: *"For behold, henceforth all generations will call me blessed"* – the one who found favour with God. Elizabeth herself, filled with the Holy Spirit, said to Mary:

(4) *"Of all women you are the most blessed, and blessed is the fruit of your womb"* (Luke 1:42).

To the wonderful message of the Angel, that she (without the knowledge of sexual relation with a man) would have a son, she said:

(5) *"I am the handmaid of the Lord, let what you have said be done to me"* (Luke 1:38).

So the Catholic Church calls Mary 'holy', 'full of grace' because the bible holds these titles for her too. The Bible says that all generations will call her blessed (Luke 1:48).

The Church does not say that Mary is the mediator between God and man. No. That is the role of Jesus, the Saviour. Mary is one of those God has saved. She, being the mother of our Saviour and God, Jesus Christ, is our mother hence we turn to her to pray for us (John 2:3). Does a mother forget the child of her womb? Just as we turn to the saints to pray for us, so also we turn to Mary to pray for us – see question 5 – Veneration of Saints. If you do not have Mary as your Mother, you cannot have Jesus as your brother.

# Q. 7 The body and soul

Some people understand the human soul to mean the body. The soul and body are two different things but both of them make up a person; one cannot exist without the other.

Here, I am not going to expound the teaching about these two realities. I am only concerned with what the Scripture says about them.

Some people have spoken so much about the soul as if that is what the Lord is interested in. The soul has been emphasised because it is the spiritual aspect of our personality.

Jesus Christ came to save the whole man and not only his soul. Read John 11:25-26; 6:35-40; 51:55-58; Paul says: ... *"we shall be changed* (1 Cor. 15:51; read also 15:42-49). It is man who will be changed – the physical will be spiritualised (1 Cor. 15:46).

Matthew reports that on the occasion of Christ's resurrection, many bodies of saints who had fallen asleep were raised (Matt. 27:52). It was Jesus who rose and his soul (Luke 24:39; John 20:27; Acts 10:41-42).

Passages where the word 'soul' is used:
(1) *"Do not be afraid of those who kill the body but cannot kill the soul"* (Matt. 10:28).
(2) *"No, Wisdom will never make its way into a crafty soul nor stay in a body that is in debt of sin"* (Wisdom 1:4).
(3) *"A body dies when it is separated from the spirit"* (James 2:26).
(4) *"... And her spirit returned and she got up at once"* (Luke 8:55).
(5) *"My soul glorifies the Lord"* (Luke 1:46).
(6) *"... A perishable body presses down the soul"* (Wisdom 9:15).
Further references: 1 Thess. 5:23; Heb. 10:38-39; 13:17; Acts 2:26-27; Wisdom 4:13-14; 3:1; Isaiah 61:10.

## Q. 8 Call no one father (Matt. 23:9)

There are those who have taken this passage literally and have concluded that Christ has ruled that the word 'father' should not be used for men. Read the passage of the Scripture where Christ said this to the disciples and you will probably understand why he said it.

I suppose Christ was not condemning the use of the word; he was however, making sure that the disciples did not become so proud with the idea that as they were chosen to teach, they merited the respectable title of Rabbis. In other words, Christ was concerned about the service and not the honour in the vocation of the disciples.

From the following passages from the Sacred Scripture, we see the use of the word 'Father'.
(1) Stephen said: "brethren and Fathers ..." (Acts 7:2).
(2) *"... in the land that long ago I gave to your fathers forever"* (Jer. 7:7; Num. 12:14).
(3) *"You shall become the father of a multitude of nations ..."* (Gen. 17:4).
Further readings: John 6:49; Philemon 1:10; Matt. 15:4-5; 23:30; Luke 1:73.

## Q. 9  Where is hell?

Luke reported one of the most interesting stories Jesus told. Please read this story in Luke 16:19-31. It is the story of the destiny of a wicked man. He was in hades, which means "hell".

Hell is a perpetual life of suffering after death. A person goes to hell simply because of the good work he refused to do – read Matt. 25:41-43. The person in hell condition will desire God but unfortunately, he will never find Him. He will have an un-quenchable thirst for God (Luke 16:24). He suffers because he has refused the invitation of Jesus: *"if any one thirst, let him come to me and drink"* – John 7:37; 4:14; 6:35; whereas those who have lived well will *"hunger no more, neither thirst any more"* (Rev. 7:16).

Hell is the loss of God one had scorned while one lived here on earth (Psalm 42:2; 63:1; 143:6). Hell is an eternal restlessness which a person suffers because he has lost that fullness of joy that he ought to have sought for, day and night, while on earth. The experience will be like that of a chicken searching for her mother.

Most Bibles use the words 'hades', 'sheol', 'fire' or 'gehenna' for hell. All of them mean the same thing: an underworld of darkness and suffering. For most of the ancient people, the above (heaven) was regarded as the home of God and His just ones; the earth is for man; and beyond the grave was regarded as a place of fire, the abode of sinners.

Passages in the Scripture where hell is mentioned: Luke 12:5; Matt. 11:23; 13:41-43; 18:9; 10:28; 23:33; 5:29-30; Mark 9:45; Wisdom 16:4; Rev. 20:10; 13-15; 2 Thess. 1:9.

## Q. 10 (a)  Where is purgatory?

Read the following passages from the Holy Scripture and think seriously about them:
(1) *"And its gates shall never be shut by day – and there shall be no night there; they shall bring into it the glory and the honour of the nations. But nothing unclean shall enter it . . ."* (Rev. 21:25-27).
(2) *"All wrongdoing is sin, but there is sin which is not mortal"* (1 John 5:17).
(3) The son of man will *"repay every man for what he has done"* (Matt. 16:27).
(4) *"This was why he had this atonement sacrifice offered for the dead, so that they might be released from their sin* (2 Maccabees 12:45).

In the above passages (2), the Scripture tells us that there are sins which are not mortal (deadly). John says that we should pray for those who have committed such sins (1 John 5:16). But what happens if such a person should die still in debt of that sin? What will be his merit? Presumably, not with hell because his sin is not deadly; not with heaven because he is still not clean; that is, he has not lived the perfect life to which he was called (Matt. 5:48). So, where should he be?

The Scripture urges us to pray that they may be released from their sin (2 Macc. 12:45).

The Jerusalem Bible says:

*"This is the only O.T. text mentioning an intermediate state where the souls of the dead are purified, and assisted in the process by the prayers of the living; i.e. purgatory"* (Jerusalem Bible, p.713).

Briefly, the term 'purgatory' which comes from the word 'purgation', is not in the Bible. It is simply the name given to that *"intermediate state where the souls of the dead are purified, and assisted by the prayers of the living"* (JB p.713; 2 Macc. 12:45).

The conclusion we can draw from the Scripture is this: God's justice will ensure that those who lived a fairly good life will not be totally condemned to hell fire; they will be paid not with hell because they have not yet paid up their debt (Matt. 5:26) but with what is in between happiness and suffering – purgatory or any name you wish.

This mid-condition will not continue for ever. When they have been purified, they will enter heaven. Purgatory will cease at the end of time. Christ has specifically revealed two conditions that will exist at the end of time – heaven and hell (Matt. 25:34, 41).

# Q. 10 (b) A startling discovery

In series of visions of angels and certain eternal dimensions, a protestant preacher discovered this intermediate state which we call Purgatory. According to the man, he told God who revealed this to him that the whole discovery was not in agreement with his theology but God told him that he was not comparing the truth he discovered with his theology. The man said:

"God also allowed me to see loved ones who had died. Then he let me see believers who were passing from this life. I saw their families in heaven being alerted by the angels that a loved one was coming home and for them to ready themselves to welcome them. Paul referred to these people as having "heavenly" or "celestial" bodies. This amplified and clarified

for me another eternal dimension. They were identifiable, and
appeared exactly the way they looked here, minus the cares,
the hurts and other problems. They were constantly experiencing tremendous joy, excitement and happiness, for heaven
is a place of continual discovery about the beauty of God!

God let me see something else I had never understood.
There is an area between our permanent abiding place in
heaven and this earth from which we can be brought back.
People who have died and have been restored to life at God's
prerogative, were still in this area. They had not yet reached
the place of their final abode. These are some very, very
interesting arrangements, but it isn't guesswork. I saw it! I
was there!

One thing God told me was so opposite to my theology
that it was hard for me to adjust my understanding to the
actual facts. I have preached that once you quit breathing,
if you are not saved, and do not know God, you have missed
heaven. God said that was not necessarily so. He said that
there is a spot where the spirit of mankind may linger for
a little time before going on to their permanent abode. Many
people who have been clinically dead know they have had this
experience. Some of them have approached the gates of hell,
have even looked in, or have been able to look into heaven,
and yet have come back. He did not try to give it in a textbook
fashion so you could prove it, or teach it as a subject, but just
as a fact! I remarked to God that this was not totally against
my theology, and he simply stated that he wasn't trying to
compare it to my theology!''

(Charles and Frances Hunter, **ANGELS ON ASSIGNMENT
as told by Roland Buck,** pp. 58-59), published by Hunter books
1602 Townhurst, Houston, Texas 7703.
God is the very Truth: He can neither deceive nor be deceived.
Let us hold to the Catholic teaching.

# Q. 11  Where is heaven?

Read the following story told by Matthew very carefully.
After six days, Jesus took with him Peter and James and John
his brother, and led them up a high mountain apart. And he
was transfigured before them, and his face shone like the sun,
and his garment became white as light. And behold, there
appeared to them Moses and Elijah, talking with him. And
Peter said to Jesus, *"Lord, it is well that we are here; if you
wish, I will make three booths here, one for you and one for*

*Moses and one for Elijah"*. He was still speaking, when a bright cloud overshadowed them, and a voice from the cloud said, *"This is my beloved Son, with whom I am well pleased, listen to him"*. When the disciples heard this, they fell on their faces, and were filled with awe ... Jesus commanded them, *"Tell no one this vision, until the son of man is raised from the dead"* (Matt. 17:1-9).

What kind of vision (experience) do you think this was? Don't you think that it was so BEAUTIFUL that Peter wanted to set up a home there? Please read 1 Peter 1:16: He and his brothers saw the glory of Jesus. It is what Christians are looking for – to see and share the glory of the risen Lord (2 Thess. 2:14). John said: *"It does not yet appear what we shall be, but we know that when he appears we shall be like him, for we shall see him as he is"* (1 John 3:2).

Our final experience of Jesus will be our experience of God; the experience of God, is an experience of heaven; for God is the heaven we are looking for.

Heaven is therefore not above or below. It is not a place. It is seeing God face to face. Heaven is an experience of God, His Angels and the glorified human beings – the saints. God, our heaven, is not just below or above; he is everywhere. He is a Spirit. The Bible says:

(1) *"In him we live and move and have our being* (Acts 17:28).

Heaven is seeing God, knowing God, and loving God. St. Augustine said that in heaven we shall see, we shall love, we shall rest – a joyful life that will never end.

God sometimes graciously permits some people to see a glimpse of heaven even before they die. The Bible bears witness to this:

(2) *"But he (Stephen), full of the Holy Spirit, gazed into heaven and saw the glory of God, and Jesus at the right hand of God ..."* (Acts 7:55-56).

"Gazed into", as used here, does not mean that God was locked up or is locked up somewhere. If God is everywhere, He was even then in, and around Stephen.

Heaven and earth are like the body and the soul in their relationships. The Body and the soul are so closely united that they cannot be physically put apart. So also heaven and earth cannot be put apart – They are very closely united (John 1:51).

So, if God permits it, we will see heaven too, even now. Heaven is in our midst. But our eyes are not open; not yet conditioned to see it. When God opens the veil we shall see everything very clearly. The Bible says:

(3) *"For now we see dimly as in a mirror, but then face to face. Now I know in part; then I shall understand fully ..."* (1 Cor. 13:12).

But the FULL experience of heaven will begin when, and only when we have taken our last breath; that is, when we have gone to the last sleep. Then and there God and man will meet; and that is heaven! It will be a sudden change. Read this story very carefully:

*There is a moving description of death-bed of one of the early members of the Carmelite reform. It runs as follows:*

Brother Albert of the Virgin, porter of the Convent of the Martyrs, was on the point of death. His countenance was aflame, and shone with a celestial light which rendered it so marvellously beautiful that all were enraptured and silently shed tears of joy ... Suddenly Brother Albert cried out in a loud voice: *"Oh! I have seen it! Oh, I have seen it! Oh, I have seen it"* and immediately lowering his arms, crossed them on his breast as he was about to close his eyes, our venerable father John of the Cross hastened to ask him this question: *"Brother Albert, what have you just seen?"* And he answered, *"Love, Love"* and remained in an ecstasy (E.L. Mascall: Grace and Glory, pp. 46-47).

The Bible says:

(4) *"Lo! I tell you a mystery. We shall not all sleep, but we shall all be changed in a moment, in the TWINKLING of an eye ..."* (1 Cor. 15:51-52).

Jesus prayed to his Father that those He has given him (Jesus) should be with him wherever he is; and that they may behold his glory (John 17:24). Heaven is seeing and loving Jesus in his glory. It can begin now in you. How? The Bible says:

(5) *"If a man loves me, he will keep my word, and my Father will love him, and we will come to him and make our HOME with HIM".* (John 14:23).

Even now, heaven has begun in us. Do you know that *"God's Spirit dwells in you?* (1 Cor. 3:16). Do you know that *"If anyone is in Christ, he is a new person; the old has passed away?"* (2 Cor. 5:17). Do you not realize Christ is in you? (2 Cor. 13:5). If Christ is in you, then the kingdom of heaven has begun in your heart. To possess Jesus through grace, is to have begun to live the life of glory – that is, the life of God. St. Thomas Aquinas said that *"grace is nothing else than a kind of beginning of glory in us".*

The kingdom is not only future, it is now. To be with Christ is to be in the kingdom. *"Where Christ is, there is heaven"* (St. John Chrysostom).

For those living in Christ, the kingdom of heaven has begun in them. They may not be aware of this. The kingdom of heaven is not some distance out of where we are at the moment. No. Heaven and earth are so closely united that they cannot be put apart as separate regions of experience. We are right in heaven but we do not know this. The Scripture says that we are living in God (Acts 17:28). But the total experience of heaven will come at our death-bed when we shall encounter Jesus in his glory. *Then and there, the kingdom will break open and we shall then know that we have been in the kingdom of heaven all these years.*

Heaven is the ultimate transfiguration of the human person at the experience of God (1 John 3:2).

## Q. 12 Has Christ other brothers?

Mary had no other child except Jesus. Some people say that Mary had another child because the evangelists (Matt. 12:46; Mark 3:31-35; Luke 8:9-21) referred to some people as the brothers of Jesus.

In the Jewish world, brothers were used for co-religionists, for example, Paul, in writing to the Corinthians, addressed them thus:

(1) *"Brothers, I myself was unable to speak to you as people of the Spirit ..."* (1 Cor. 3:1).

Obviously, the whole Christian community in Corinth was not of the same father and mother with Paul. In Genesis 13:8, Abraham called Lot his brother, but we know that they were not the same father and mother. For their relations, read Genesis 11:27.

In Nigeria, we also know that people with a claim to one ancestor call themselves brothers and sisters.

Jerusalem Bible, commenting on Matt. 12:46, says *"Not Mary's children but near relations, cousins perhaps which both Hebrew and Aramaic style "brothers"* (JB p.35).

Read the following passages from the Holy Scripture where the word 'brother' is used: Matt. 5:22; 7:3-4; 18:15; 35; 28:10; Acts 2:29; 3:17; 7:1-2. In most of these places you will see the word 'brethren' used. Further reference *"Brother Saul, ... regain your sight..."* (Acts 9:17); ... *"warn him as a brother"* (2 Thess. 3:15; Gal. 1:19) see who James was (Matt. 20:2-33; Mark 1:19).

## Q. 13 (a) Why holy days of obligation
### (Easter, Christmas, etc ...)

Some people say that since the words 'Easter' and 'Christmas' are not in the Bible, those who observe these feasts are doing something contrary to the Bible. No, they are not doing something contrary to the Bible as long as they are observing them in honour of the Lord. Listen to what the Scripture says:

(1) *"If one man keeps certain days as holier than others, and another considers all days equally holy, each must be left free to hold his own opinion"* (Romans 14:5-7).

St. Paul went on to say that each person who does so, does it in honour of the Lord. Therefore, when the Catholic Church sets aside certain days of the year for the remembrance of some aspect of our Lord's life, she does so in honour of the Lord.

The Words 'Christmas' or 'Easter' are certainly not in the Bible. They are just names given to the feasts which commemorate the birth and the resurrection of Christ.

The other argument by some people is that Jesus was not born on the 25th day of December or that he did not rise on the Easter Sunday. Historians are not agreed on the date of Christ's birth or resurrection. However, the Church has, after the most serious historical research, decided to celebrate the feasts on the days we now have them. The important thing nevertheless, is not the days; the important thing is that the feasts are celebrated in honour of the Lord. This would be the view of Paul (Romans 14:5-7).

# Q. 13 (b) Are you saved?

God wants all men to be saved (1 Thess. 4:3; 1 Tim. 2:4; 2 Peter 3:9) and that was why He sent His only begotten son, Jesus. To be saved, one has to (first and foremost) believe in God (Heb. 11:6) and in the Lord Jesus Christ (Act 16:31).

But believing in Jesus is not a question of saying *"Lord! Lord!"* Please read Matt. 7:21; nor can anyone, while still living in the present life, be absolutely sure that he is already saved. Listen to what the Bible says:

(1) *"An athlete is not crowned unless he completes according to the rules"* (2 Tim. 2:5). The question you might ask yourself is: Have I completed the race according to the rules? In spite of Paul's experience of Christ, he still said that he had not won his salvation. Listen carefully to him:

(2) *"Not that I have already obtained this or am already perfect; but I press on to make it my own, because Christ Jesus has made me his own".*

*Brethren, I do not consider that I have made it my own, I press on toward the goal for the prize of the upward call of God in Christ Jesus"* (Phil. 3:12-15).

Again Paul advises us:

(3) *". . . work out your salvation with fear and trembling"* (Phil. 2:12).

There are good reasons why we should work out our salvation with fear and trembling. These are:

(4) We are still sinners. *"If we say that we have no sin in us, we are deceiving ourselves and refusing to admit the truth ... To say that we have never sinned is to call God a liar"* (1 John 1:8-10).

(5) We have this gift of salvation in *"earthen vessels, to show that the transcendent power belongs to God and not to us"* (2 Cor. 4:7).

So, it is not those who say *"Jesus! Jesus!"* that will be saved (Matt. 7:21-22). To be saved, we need to believe in Jesus and do good works; for faith without good work is useless (James 2:14-26; Gal. 5:6).

## Q. 14 The Bible does not contain everything we believe

John writes to the Church:

(1) *"There are several things I have to tell you, but I have thought it best not to trust them to PAPER and INK. I hope instead to visit you and talk to you PERSONALLY so that our joy may be complete"* (2 John 1:12).

This was the very John that Jesus asked to take care of Mary (John 19:26-27).

Paul writes to the Thessolonians:

(2) *"... hold to the traditions which you were taught by us, either by WORD OF MOUTH or by letter"* (2 Thess 2:15).

Other references: 2 Thess 3:6; 1 Cor. 11:2; John 21:25.

A tradition is a belief or practice which is handed down to a people from their ancestors. The Christian traditions which the Church asks us to believe are those doctrines with divine authority but not committed to writing. The Catholic Church is in possession of these traditions which she received from the apostolic successors. She (on the authority of the Bible) accepts these unwritten beliefs and practices as part of revelation. Paul tells the Church at Corinth: *"...maintain the traditions even as I have delivered them to you"* (1 Cor. 11:2). Read also 2 Tim. 1:13.

So whatever the Church does, she has the support of the Bible and the tradition handed on to her from the time of the Apostles. *"Christianity can never become a mere book religion"* (Vat. 2:11).

## Q. 15 The assumption of the Blessed Virgin Mary

The Catholic Church says that Mary was assumed into heaven. Which means that she who bore our saviour and God, did not see corruption. This is an example of a tradition which the Catholic Church teaches and asks us to believe. Mary, the Church says, *"was exalted by the Lord as Queen of all, in order that she might be the more thoroughly conformed to her son, the Lord of Lords* (Apoc. 19:16) and the conqueror of sin and death" (Vat. 2).

The Fathers of the Church, the great Doctors, and ancient writers had all in their writings and sermons talked about Mary's assumption into the heavenly glory. *"All these Fathers base their conclusions on the Bible, which has given us the picture of our Lord's Mother as inseparably attached to her divine son, and constantly sharing his lot"* (Breviary – Feast of Assumption).

Mary was trusted to the care of John (John 19:26-27). The Bible does not say more than this. But John tells the Church:

> *There are several things I have to tell you, but I have thought it best not to trust it to PAPER and INK. I hope instead to visit you and talk to you personally so that our joy may be complete"* (2 Jn. 1:12; 3 Jn. 1:13).

The Catholic Church believes both in the Bible and in the unwritten beliefs and practices handed on to her from the Apostles. We believe in the assumption of the Blessed Virgin Mary because the Church who is the Custodian of the Sacred truth (Eph. 3:10) teaches it.

Further reference: Rev. 12:1. This is John's writing about a woman who appeared in the sky clothed with the Sun (some Bible Scholars apply this both to the Church and to Mary) which the Church reads at the Liturgy (Mass) of Assumption of Mary.

## Q. 16 Do we need teachers in the Church?

Some people might say that we do not need priests to teach others about God. Everyone can teach. Of course, everyone can teach if everyone knows what to teach. Does the Scripture not say that all will be taught by God (John 6:45; Jeremiah 31:34)? But the Bible says that some are called specifically to teach.

(2) *"Let not many of you become teachers"* (James 3:1).

(3) *"Then Jesus said to the crowds and to his disciples: "The Scribes and Pharisees sit on Moses' seat; so practise and observe whatever they tell you . . ."* (Matt. 23:1-37).

Further reference: 1 Cor. 12:28. The different kinds of gifts in the Church.

The task of interpreting the word of God as it should be interpreted (the word of God whether written or handed on) has been *"entrusted exclusively to the living teaching office of the Church, whose authority is exercised in the name of Jesus Christ"* (Vat. 2). Read also Eph. 3:10. The Bible is not therefore to be interpreted in the way one likes it. (cf. Questions 43 and 44).

# Q. 17 Who is the Father and Mother of Jesus? Mary is the only human parent of Jesus

This question looks funny because any human person must have parents; but the question as to who are the earthly parents of Jesus, is not a funny one because Jesus does not tell us or give us the impression that he has, for example, an earthly father. All through John's gospel, he claims to have come from heaven and often and on, declaring God as his father. John emphasises this fact more than any other evangelist. The points to bear in mind are these:

### The father of Jesus - Popular view among the Jews:

John records two occasions only when people called Joseph the father of Jesus. But this is the people's view, not John's view (John 1:45-46; 6:42). John never says that Joseph is the father of Jesus. What he recorded were people's opinion about Jesus' parenthood: which of course, does not mean that he agreed with the people's opinion.

The Jews, as a matter of fact, almost called Jesus a bastard (John 8:19; 49; 9:29). All these show that even the Jews too were not clear as to who was the father of Jesus.

Jesus says that God is his father (John 8:41-59). He never refers to any human person as his father. John, though does not talk about the earthly father of Jesus, talks about the 'brothers' of Jesus (John 2:12; 7:3, 5-6, 10). John does not use this word in its strict sense, otherwise he would not deny any human father to Jesus. For the Jews, the term 'brother' is used for a co-RELIGIONIST or a NEAR RELATION. For example, Abram called Lot his brother (Genesis 13:8) but we know from the Bible that they were really not brothers (Gen. 11:27). Similarly, Paul called James the Lord's brother (Gal. 1:19) but we know too from the Bible that James and John were sons of Zebedee (Mark 1:19). Mary is the mother of Jesus. According to John, Mary is the Mother of Jesus (John 2:1-5; 12:19, 25-26). Paul links Jesus human origin with only a woman (Gal. 4:4) but leaves to talk about his human father. For Paul, Jesus is the Son of God (Rom. 8:3; Gal. 4:4).

Our conclusion is this: For John, Jesus has a mother but his father is God.

# Q. 18 Mary's double blessing

As we mentioned already (see question 17) for John (even as well as Paul – Gal. 4:4), the human origin of Jesus is linked only with Mary; the father of Jesus being God (John 8:41-59). Mary is mentioned as the mother of Jesus four times in the gospel (John 2:1-5; 12; 6:42; 19:25-28). But in all these, she is never mentioned by name. Scripture does not say why John does not want to call Mary by her name. It could be an act of respect or the custom of the people. Even the Lord himself addressed her as 'woman'; a word which, as an address, is not disrespectful. *"It was commonly employed in speaking to women* (John 4:21). *In its use, it resembles our formal address "madam".*

As for the ministry of Christ, Mary appeared at two significant occasions –

(1) When Jesus first manifested his glory (John 2:11) but this early manifestation of glory was at the intervention of Mary (John 2:4-5).

(2) Mary appeared again when her son was on the cross. She was there when her son, the only son, was right on the cross and Jesus saw her agony (I say agony because in spite of her fullness of grace, we cannot imagine her enjoying seeing her son suffering and dying on the cross – our Blessed mother is not a sadist) and then Jesus handed her over to the disciple whom he loved (John 19:26-27). We cannot push Mary aside as we talk about Jesus because:

   (a) Mary is the mother of God through her faith-acceptance of the word delivered to her from God. John and even Elizabeth points out her exemplary faith (John 2:5; Luke 1:45).

   (b) Mary has a double blessing of being the mother of the redeemer (Luke 1:43) and the one who heard God's word and kept it firmly in her heart (Luke 11:27-28). In conclusion, we can therefore say this:

      (i) That in the work of redemption, Mary continues that work of intercession which she had already begun in Cana even when the Son had clearly expressed that it was not his time to manifest who he was (John 2:4).

      (ii) Mary gave the Word-made-man that humanity he had. *"The Church is ever mindful (even in using the material elements of bread and wine to efficaciously make present the body and blood of Christ in the Eucharist) that it was the flesh of the Virgin Mary which originally made present Jesus Christ, whole and entire, in the form of our humanity"* (CRUX 1 March, 1976).

If we have the spirit of Mary, we will possess Jesus equally as she did but who among us can say to God with our whole mind and heart *"Let it be done to me according to your word"* (Luke 1:38)? Only Mary did so.

# Q. 19 (a) Why do we baptize infants? Does the Bible condemn infant baptism?

(a) No. The Bible does not condemn infant baptism. The Bible does not even talk about the age at which a person should be baptized.

(b) Jesus brought us the fullness of life (John 10:10) and he himself said that through the WATERS of baptism and the gift of the Holy Spirit, this new life will be given (John 3:3; 5). To be born anew, Jesus does not say that one has to be of a particular age.

(c) Whoever that is born into this world therefore needs the new life; he or she needs salvation (Rom. 6:3-4; 1 Peter 3:21; 2 Cor. 5:17) in spite of his or her age. Some people are like the disciples who never wanted children to be brought to Christ (Matt. 19:13-14). Jesus told the disciples: 'Let the children come to me, and do not hinder them' (Matt. 19:14). So, those who say that children should not be baptized, are saying in effect that children should not have the new life which Jesus brought to every human person. Every person who has soul and body needs the life of God (John 3:3, 5; 4:14).

(d) We read in the Bible of certain entire households entering the faith AND THIS MUST HAVE MEANT CHILDREN AS WELL AS ADULTS (Acts 16:15, 35; 18:8). Helpful statements by reputed theologians on this issue:

(e) St. John Chrysostom says: *"This is why we baptize infants even though they have not sinned: that there may be added to them justice, filiation ("Sonship" – my own words), inheritance, grace to be brothers and members of Christ and to become dwelling places of the Holy Spirit".*

(f) The Council of Trent says: *"If anyone says that no one is to be baptized except at the age which Christ was baptized, or at the hour of death, let him be anathema".*

*"If any one says that because infants do not make an act of faith, they are not to be numbered among the faithful after they receive baptism, and moreover, that they are to be rebaptized when they come to the use of reason; or if any one says that it is better to omit the baptism of infants rather than baptize them, merely in the faith of the Church, let him be anathema".*

*"If anyone says that when these baptized infants grow up they are to be asked whether they wish to ratify what their sponsors promised in their name at baptism; and if they answer in the negative, they are to be left to their own judgment, and that until they come to their senses . . . let him be anathema".* Pope Paul VI, in his Credo of June 30, 1973, wrote:

*"We believe in one baptism instituted by our Lord Jesus Christ for the remission of sin. Baptism should be administered even to LITTLE CHILDREN who have not yet been able to be guilty of any PERSONAL SIN, in order that though born deprived of supernatural grace, they may be reborn of water and the Holy Spirit to the divine life in Christ Jesus".*

Take note of the argument of our holy Father. I find it very strong. It agrees very much with my point on page 18, Nos. (b) and (c). My emphasis has been and is still, the need for the new life through Jesus Christ (Rom. 6:23). The kingdom of God is for all whether young or old.

1. The priest, edited by Jordan Auman, O.P. Vol. 129, No. 3; pp. 18-21; March 1973.

## Q. 19 (b) How was baptism done by the early Christians?

Baptism is an immersion, a dipping into water, a washing away of sin. It is an action of Christ through the Ministry of the priest. The symbolism of water is a sign of purification and new life; a new relationship with God (Romans 6:1-11; Eph. 2:155ff; 2 Cor. 5:17ff).

The question is: how was baptism done at the time of John the Baptizer and the early Christians? Certainly, at the time of John the Baptizer, the method was a dipping into water (John 3:22-23). John's baptism was however, not a Christian baptism and does not have to become the Christian ways of baptizing. John's baptism introduced a man into the people of Israel; people regarded as then belonging to Abraham, saved therefore from the anger of God and were waiting for the Messiah who was to come (Matt. 3:7-10; Mark 1:4).

Jesus did not baptize anybody with water (see John 4:1-2). So, he did not give us an example. Jesus did point out two important things for baptism: a person ought to be baptized 'In the name of the Father and of the Son and of the Holy Spirit' (Matt. 28:19) and with water (John 3:5). Should such a person be dipped into water, washed with water or sprinkled with water? Jesus did not give us an example.

The early Christians might have taken over the Jewish form of baptism by immersion but from the account of the CROWDS of persons and individual persons baptized (Acts 2:41; 61:27-33; 10:44-47; 18:8; 16:14-15) we are not told that these baptisms were done in rivers in the way John the Baptist did baptize people.

Baptism by immersion is good but if that is not possible, at least a sprinkling of water over the head, is also good as we read in DIDACHE 7:3. The Didache is a collection of some of the early practices of the infant Church.

## Q. 20 Does the Bible condemn any food or drink? (cf. Question 36)

The Bible certainly condemns any kind of indulgence: over-eating or over-drinking (drunkenness). The Bible is concerned with those who eat, drink and enjoy themselves so much that they forget themselves, forget God, forget the good life and in that bad condition, sin against God and man. So the Bible condemns excessive enjoyment. Read Luke 21:34; Gal. 5:21; Rom. 13:13; Isaiah 22:13; 1 Cor. 15:32. The kingdom of God is not food and drink. It is right living, Joy, Peace in the Holy Spirit (Rom. 14:17).

However, eating and drinking are not bad human acts (Rom. 14:6, 14). The Bible does not condemn food or wine. Paul, the Apostle, even recommended a little wine for the health of Timothy (1 Tim. 5:23). He was against unnecessary rules about food and drink (Col. 2:20-23). On the whole, the spiritual law is: *"Don't get drunk with wine"* (Eph. 5:18).

Nevertheless, God loves us whether we eat or we do not eat (1 Cor. 8:8). The Bible says:

*"So whether you eat or drink, or whatever you do, do all to the glory of God"* (1 Cor. 10:31).

The important spiritual advice is: Control your stomach so that you do not become a slave of any pleasure; for one of the fruits of the Holy Spirit is self-control (Gal. 5:23; 2 Tim. 1:7).

## Q. 21 Why did God create the devil? Why does God not, if he is all good, destroy the devil?
Read Jude 1:6

Catholics believe that the devil is an angelic person whose will is fixed forever in evil. When God created the angels, He made them good and gave them a share in His own divine life. But before they could enter heaven, they were tested by God. Some of the angels failed the test and sinned grievously against God. They are called evil spirits or *"fallen angels"*. Their leader is named Satan (which in Hebrew means the Enemy), Lucifer or simply the devil.

The devil is a spiritual being who has no body and that is why we cannot see him. Because he has intelligence and free

25

will, he is a personal being. He is evil through his own fault. He was good when created by God, but he freely made himself evil by abusing his freedom.

The devil is under God's control and cannot act without God's permission. He is allowed to incite us to sin (temptation), to enter human bodies and move the imagination and locomotive faculties (diabolical possession). However, he has no power over our free will. He can never force our consent to evil. Although the devil is clever and as a roaring lion, goes about seeking someone to devour" (1 Pt. 5:8), we should not be afraid of him for, *"God is faithful and will not permit you to be tempted beyond your strength, but with the temptation will also give you a way out that you may be able to bear it"* (1 Cor. 10:13).

If God destroyed the devil, he would violate the precious gift of freedom and deprive man of opportunities for virtue and merit. To destroy free beings would mean God's failure to fulfil the plan of creation. Besides, it is a far greater punishment for the devil to suffer eternally than to be snuffed out of existence. As the last, God will take from him all power and trust him back, hopeless and helpless into hell forever.

## Q. 22 How do you prove from the Bible that the Catholic Church has the power to forgive sins?

Christ promised St. Peter and the Apostles the power to forgive sins (Matt. 16:18, 18), and fulfilled that promise on the first Easter evening (John 20:21-23).

The power of the keys implied supreme jurisdiction over the whole Church and necessarily included the power to forgive sin, because sin alone excludes men from the kingdom of heaven. God ratified this power in St. Peter, the other Apostles and their successors, when he said *"Whatever you shall bind on earth should be bound in heaven, and whatever you shall loose on earth shall be loosed in heaven"* (Matt. 16:19).

This promise was fulfilled when Christ said, *"As the Father has sent Me I also send you".* When He had said this, He breathed upon them and said to them, *"Receive the Holy Spirit; whose sins you shall forgive, they are forgiven them; and whose sins you shall retain, they are retained"* (John 20:21-23).

Why has the Father sent Him? To save sinners by pardoning their sins. *"I have come to call sinners, not the just"* (Matt. 9:13). *"I was not sent except to the lost sheep of the house of Israel"* (Matt. 15:24). *"The son of Man came to save what was lost"* (Matt. 18:11). *"Jesus Christ came into the world to save sinners"* (1 Tim. 1:14).

He frequently pardoned sinners; namely, Magdalen (Luke 7:47), the woman in adultery (John 8:11), Zacchaeus (Luke 19:9), the man sick of the palsy (Matt. 9:2), the thief on the Cross (Luke 23:43). The pardoning power which He exercised, He bestowed upon His Apostles. As the Father sent Him to Pardon, so He sent them to pardon in His name, *"Receive the Holy Spirit"*, said Christ because forgiving sin implies the giving of the spiritual life of grace to the sinner, and making him a temple of the Holy Spirit (1 Cor. 5:16).

St. Augustine says: *"Let no one say: I confess my sins secretly to God, it is enough that He who is to forgive me knows the penance I make in my heart. If this were the case, Jesus would not have sent the Lepers (Lk. 17:11-14) to the Priests nor would He have said to the Apostles: That which you will loose on earth will be loosed in Heaven. If God had given us the power to open Heaven by Ourselves, His having given the keys to the Church would be useless. It is not enough to confess ourselves to God, therefore, but we must confess ourselves to those who received from Him the power to loose and bind".*

Sins are not to be pardoned lightly, but only after careful judging of the disposition of the sinner. If he is sorry for his sins, he is forgiven by the Apostles and by God; if he refuses to repent, his sins are not forgiven by the Apostles, or by God. They are retained.

Was this pardoning power to cease with the Apostles? By no means. The very nature of the Church, which is the representative of Christ to continue His work until the end of the world (Matt. 28:20), proves that the pardoning power was not a personal gift to the Apostles, but a permanent institution to last as long as there were sinners in the world (Council of Trent).

# Q. 23 Astrology is about the stars and the influence they have on human beings and human affairs; and the foretelling of early events by the very position of the stars. Why does the Catholic Church condemn astrology?

Astrology is a superstitious practice (Superstition. Def: A person seeks to obtain from a creature, stars, dreams, some information or benefits which can be obtained from God alone) which encourages the teaching that all things are subject to fate. It teaches that the occurrences of events is fixed in advance for all times in such a manner that human beings are powerless to change them. Events are inevitable, cannot be avoided ... and are certain to happen. This teaching leads to the denial of Divine Providence.

Human life is thus regulated by the course of the stars and planets irrespective of man's free will and God's grace.

The stars exercise absolutely no determining influence on human lives or human affairs. To place any belief in a horoscope in order to foretell one's future is absolute nonsense. St. Augustine attacked this teaching strongly in his book, City of God (Bk. 8; Chapt. 19) and St. Thomas Aquinas, great Dominican Theologian, writes, *"If anyone applies the observation of the stars in order to know with certitude future human actions, his conduct is based on a false and vain opinion (Summa, IIa IIae, q.45 a5).*

## Q. 24 If it is superstitious to believe in dreams, why does God make use of dreams to make known his will to men both in the old and the new testament?

Our daily life and our daily conduct should be guided by a rightly instructed conscience ... and not by dreams. Sacred Scripture frequently warns us *"not to observe dreams"*, and teaches that *"dreams have deceived many, and many persons have failed who have put their trust in them"* (Lev. 19:26; Deut. 18:10; Sirach 34:7). Ordinarily, dreams have a natural cause; our imagination forms *"pictures"* from the scattered events of our daily life. ... In our dreams, these events are usually not reasonably correct; they are distorted and often absurd and nonsensical. Psychologists and doctors tell us that the contents of our dreams depend much on the state of our health, our nerves, our fears, and the position we are in while we are sleeping.

On the other hand, God has communicated with people by means of dreams. Abimelech, Jacob, Solomon, Nebuchadnezzar, Daniel, St. Joseph and St. Paul experienced prophetic dreams (Gen. 28:12; 31:10; 3 Kings 3:5-15; Dan. 2:19; 7:1; Matt. 1:20; 2:13, Acts 23:11; 27:23). We should not forget, however, that these persons were also experiencing natural dreams to which they paid no attention.

When God is the cause of our dreams, He always takes care to make their supernatural character evident. In other words, when God is the cause of our dreams, we will KNOW it without a doubt.

## Q. 25 Why are not all our prayers answered as the Lord promised?
### (John 14:13)

If we pray humbly (Ps. 1:10; Luke 11:5-8) and perseveringly (Matt. 14:22-28; Luke 11:5-13; 18:1-7) for spiritual blessings that will ensure our soul's salvation – the grace to resist temptation, the pardon of sin, and the grace of final perseverance – God will answer us.

If we ask spiritual blessings for others, God will pour forth His grace in abundant measure, but the sinner we pray for may resist God's grace even to the end. God will never force the human will, for He demands a free, not a forced service.

If we pray for temporal blessings, such as health, success, and fortune, God may grant our prayer by denying what we ask. We must always pray in accordance with the divine plan. Our Lord gave us the example in the Garden of Gethsemane when He prayed, *"Father, if it is possible, let this cup pass away from Me; yet, not as I will, but as You will"* (Matt. 26:39).

If sickness were to bring us close to God, and health make us forgetful of Him; if failure were to humble us, and success make us proud and arrogant; if poverty (poorness) were to make us followers of the poor Christ (1 Cor. 8:9) and riches were to cause us to abandon the faith – ought not God in His mercy and love refuse us what we in our ignorance are asking? A mother who loves her child will not give her child a sharp knife to play with no matter how hard he cries for it. A good doctor will not change the medicine he is giving the patient if he knows it will thereby cause his death.

## Q. 26 How can an infinitely good and merciful God condemn whom he loves to the everlasting torments of hell?

Hell is indeed a great mystery, and like every other mystery of Christianity, it is beyond the scope of any human mind. The Catholic know that it is a teaching, divinely revealed by God and he accepts it humbly and without question on the word of

Jesus Christ, the Son of God. As St. Paul says, "HOW IN-COMPREHENSIBLE ARE HIS JUDGMENTS AND HOW UNSEARCHABLE HIS WAYS" (Rom. 11:33).

The unbeliever asks, "How can a good God punish His creatures in hell?" and at the same time asks, "How can a world so full of sinfulness and misery be the creation of an infinitely wise and good God". According to the unbeliever, God is either too good, or too evil, and so he denies that there is hell or a divine providence. And yet in God all is one . . . His mercy, justice, power and love. Because our human intellects are limited, we set one attribute of God against another. God cannot defeat His mercy by His justice, nor can He defeat His justice by His mercy. He cannot deviate from the right without ceasing to be God. He is justice. He is mercy.

The Church has always taught that if a man is condemned to hell, he has certainly deserved it. If he can say honestly I did not know God's law or I could not help sinning, God cannot or will not punish him. For God *"wishes all men to be saved"* (1 Tim. 2:4). If a man dies with his will rebellious to God, HE PUTS HIMSELF IN HELL. He is responsible . . . not God.

There are persons who have deliberately chosen to corrupt the innocent. There are persons who have constantly stolen large sums of money. There are persons who have deliberately taken the lives of people in murder. There are persons who have cheated innocent people out of all their money and property. Can God, Jesus Christ, justly say to those persons, if they die unrepentant, *"Come blessed of my Father, take possession of the Kingdom prepared for you from the foundation of the world?"* (Matt. 25:24).

Satan would indeed triumph over Christ if he could promise heaven to those who led perfectly sinful lives. Hell implies his defeat, for it vindicates the supremacy of Christ and the divine law which cannot be defied without punishment.

# Q. 27 Is baptism in the Holy Spirit another sacrament? (cf. Question 56)

Baptism in the Holy Spirit is not another sacrament. The Sacrament which gives us the fullness of God's Spirit is called Confirmation (Acts 8:14-17; 19:1-7). Every Catholic who has been confirmed has received the Holy Spirit whole and entire. The Bible says: God does not ration his gift of the Spirit (John 3:34).

What then is the Baptism in the Holy Spirit? For most people, the term 'Baptism in the Holy Spirit' is a description of what people experience when they are prayed upon or when hands are laid upon them in the name of Jesus, so that they might receive the gifts of the Holy Spirit dwelling within them. We know that the Holy Spirit is already dwelling within the baptized and confirmed Christian. The Bible says: *"You must know that your body is a temple of the Holy Spirit, who is within – the Spirit you have received from God"* (1 Cor. 6:19).

When a person receives the Baptism of the Holy Spirit, either through the prayers of others or by praying for himself, he experiences as a result of it, a change in his relation to the Spirit – he experiences a new sense of the presence of God in his life.

A good number of Christians are really not alive in Jesus Christ. They are not active. They are not able to do good. Therefore, the result of receiving the 'Baptism of the Spirit' is a new relationship with the Holy Spirit. 'Baptism of the Holy Spirit' is a renewal of the whole man an experience of the presence and power of God within the confirmed Christian; a presence and power which the Christian had never experienced.

The Bible tells us: *"Do not grow slack but fervent in Spirit"* (Roman 12:11). Ephesians 4:23 says: *"Be renewed in Spirit of your mind"* This renewal in the Spirit (Spiritual revolution – Eph. 4:23-24) is the aim of the 'Baptism in the Holy Spirit'.

Further readings – For the powers which the Holy Spirit confers on the Christian, read Romans 12:6-8; Eph. 4:11; 1 Cor. 12:8-11; 27-28. For the fruit of the Spirit, read Galatians 5:22, John 15:8.

The Bible tells us: *"Never try to suppress the Spirit"* (1 Thess. 5:19).

# Q. 28  Why do Catholic priests not marry?

The Bible has this to say about remaining unmarried: *"Some men are incapable of sexual activity from birth; some have been deliberately made so; and some there are who have freely renounced sex for the sake of God's reign"* (Matt. 19:12). They have freely and joyously accepted to remain single for the sake of the kingdom of heaven.

The Bible says: *"I should like you to be free of all worries. The unmarried man is busy with the Lord's affairs, concerned with pleasing the Lord; but the married man is busy with this world's demands and occupied with pleasing his wife. This means he is divided ... The Virgin is concerned with the things of the Lord, in pursuit of holiness in body and spirit"* (1 Cor. 7:32-35).

The Catholic priest does not marry because he wants to devote his whole time to the service of the Lord. He does not want to be divided. He remains unmarried for the sake of the Kingdom of God to dedicate his whole life to the service of others.

This is not to say that marriage is bad. No, marriage is good and some are called to it. The Catholic priest by remaining unmarried, wants to follow the footsteps of his Lord and Master, Jesus Christ. Jesus was not married. St. Paul was not married and he would be glad if everyone else had this gift, but the fact is that all do not, for God gives some the grace of continence and others the grace of marriage (1 Cor. 7:7).

Some people say that a man cannot live without a woman. My answer is that it is possible to live without a woman, and without having sex. The Bible says: *". . . for God all things are possible"* (Matthew 19:26). God has power to make a person chaste. He says: *". . . for my yoke is easy and my burden light"* (Matt. 11:30).

When the Catholic priest accepts to remain unmarried for the sake of the gospel, God to whom he has given his whole life, will give him the power to remain chaste. The Bible says: *"In him who is the source of my strength I have strength for everything"* (Philippians 4:13). And again, the Bible says: *". . . where the Spirit of the Lord is there is freedom"* (2 Cor. 3:17). God has the power to make a person free from sexual passion. St. Augustine says: *"God does not order things which are impossible, but while He commands, He advises us to do what we can and to ask for that which we cannot do, then He helps us, so that we can practise it".* For man, it is impossible to remain unmarried, and without sexual experience, but with God's assistance, this is possible.

# Q. 29 (a) Are there harmful doctrines?

In view of the fact that some Catholics go outside the Catholic Church to pick up whatever doctrines they find in other religious bodies, most often to their own detriment, it is important that we point out to them the danger of shopping around for diluted (watered-down) doctrines.

Let us consider some questions which reflect some of the beliefs of some of those religious groups; for according to them, they are the only ones in good standing with the Lord, other people outside their groups, are not saved. Our questions are:

(A)   Can one claim to be saved while still living in the flesh?

(B)  Is the Bible against the Blessed Virgin Mary?
     Why are some religious groups against her?

(C)  Are visions, revelations, signs and wonders, proof that a religious sect has the truth?

(D) Does the Bible support the view that every unbaptized person is an enemy of God and therefore will not be saved?

We shall examine these questions in the present comprehensive edition because so many errors arise from their discussion. Here in the introduction, I will only deal with some of the preliminary issues and touch on some essential points in them, reserving a detailed discussion of each of them to its appropriate section.

The danger of following false doctrines is pointed out by Plato in his *Protagoras*. *Protagoras* is a dialogue in which Plato the wise, points out 'inter alia', the great danger of allowing people to fill our minds and our tongues with their poisonous doctrines. In the dialogue, Socrates tells Hippocrates that there is a difference between buying an edible thing and buying people's opinions. When you buy an edible thing, you can carry it home and get those who know something about nutrition to examine it to see if it is good for consumption; but this is not the case with doctrines. When one goes to buy a doctrine from any teacher, one carries it home in one's soul (inside oneself) and if the doctrine is a bad one, the buyer is already infected with something dangerous. Read the dialogue and think about it:

**Hippocrates:** "With what is a soul nourished?

**Socrates:** With doctrines, presumably, and we must take care, my good friend, that the sophist, in commending his wares, does not deceive us, as both merchant and dealer do in the case of our bodily food. For among the provisions, you know, in which these men deal, not only are they themselves ignorant of what is good or bad for the body since in selling they commend them all, but the people who buy from them are so too, unless one happens to be a trainer or a doctor. And in the same way, those who take their doctrines the round of our cities, hawking them about to any odd purchaser who desires them, commend everything that they sell, and there may well be some of these too, my good sir, who are ignorant which of their wares is good or bad for the soul; and in just the same case are the people who buy from them, unless one happens to have a doctor's knowledge here also, but of the soul. So then, if you are well informed as to what is good or bad among these wares, it will be safe for you to buy doctrines from Protagoras or from anyone else you please: but if not, take care, my dear fellow, that you do not risk your greatest treasure on a toss of the dice. *For I tell you there is far more serious risk in the purchase of doctrines than in that of eatables.*

When you buy victuals and liquors, you can carry them off from the dealer or merchant in separate vessels, and before you take them into your body by drinking or eating, you can lay them by in your house and take the advice of an expert whom you can call in, as to what is fit to eat or drink and what is not, and how much you should take and when; so that in this purchase, the risk is not serious. But you cannot carry away doctrines in a separate vessel: you are compelled, when you have handed over the price, to take the doctrine in your very soul by learning it, and so to depart either an injured or a benefited man. These, then, are questions which we have to consider with the aid of our elders, since we ourselves are still rather young to unravel so great a matter. (Protagoras 313D-314EB, Pp. 107-109).

## Q. 29 (b) Are there cases of those who have suffered on account of false doctrine?

Yes, there are. Few years ago, an American Evangelist Rev. Jim Jones of the People's Temple, seduced over 900 people to live with him in the jungles of Guyana. Members of this organisation, the PEOPLE'S TEMPLE, were suspicious of almost everyone who did not belong to their group. In their Community located in the jungles of Guyana, a U.S. Congressman, Leo Ryan, and about 5 pressmen were put to death. The men had gone to investigate the Community's activities. After their death, Jones got the entire community, over 900 of them to drink poison which killed them. They died as a result of false doctrine.

Who was Jones? What did he teach? Some of his teachings were true and some were false. Jones was a self-appointed leader and Messiah, with a socialist vision. Jones' Society believes in the integration of black and white Americans and in the principle of justice (fairness). Jones' group were anti-racism and in favour of humanitarian good work. They believed in common life but they also believed in common death. To his crowded assemblage, Jones said on the day of their death: "We must die with dignity". That these people should believe that dying together by suicide was right and it was dying with dignity was a serious error.

How was Jones able to get such a following? Why were they all totally obedient to him to the point of accepting suicide on that large scale? The answer of course comes from the techniques of indoctrination. In Nigeria we call it brainwashing. Having shown how false doctrine works, we must ask ourselves another question:

## (A) Can one claim to be saved while still living in the flesh?

By "flesh" here is meant, man in his concrete existence. The Bible says that after this life, we shall not have the kind of bodies we have now (1 Cor. 15:42-57). This raises the questions:

(a) What does it mean (at least for us now with bodies) to be Saved?
(b) Would a person who is Saved still experience pain (physical or mental), fear, dread, anxiety, worry?
(c) Would he still need to take precaution against devilish powers (Eph. 6:10-20; 1 Pt. 5:8)?
(d) Would a person who is Saved still be sensitive to insults and impoliteness of any kind?
(e) Would a person who is Saved experience the rebellion of the flesh – strong desire for food, drink and sex?

If your answer to any of the above questions is "Yes", it is clear that you have not got your "complete freedom" which is one meaning of Salvation. Then you can say with Paul:

"I do not claim that I have already succeeded or have already become perfect. I keep striving to win the prize for which Christ Jesus has already won me to himself. Of course, my brothers, I really do not think that I have already won it; the one thing I do, however, is to forget what is behind me and do my best to reach what is ahead. So I run straight towards the goal in order to win the prize, which is God's call through Christ Jesus to the life above. All of us who are spiritually mature should have the same attitude. But if some of you have a different attitude, God will make this clear to you" (Phil. 3:12-16).

Since we are running towards the goal, we cannot claim that we have arrived. An object is not in its place of rest if it is still rolling. If we take St. Paul's letter as a whole, we see him talking about two ideas of salvation:

(i) We are Saved (2 Tim. 1:9-10; 1 Pt. 1:3; Eph. 2:4-22).
(ii) We are waiting to be Saved (1 Pt. 1:4; Rom. 8:23-25; Eph. 1:14).

In the passage of Scripture cited above (Phil. 2:12-16), St. Paul points out:

(i) that he has not succeeded.
(ii) that he has not become perfect, i.e. he is not exactly what he should be – he has not attained his wholeness, complete freedom (Eph. 1:14; Gal. 5:5).

(iii) that he runs towards the goal to win the prize.

St. Paul is aware that he does not have the "prize" at hand yet. This of course, means that salvation is yet to come, although Christ has won it for him.

Considering all these things, it would be presumptuous to say without qualification: "I am Saved". We shall come back to this issue in its appropriate section, to make a detailed discussion of it.

The second question we might consider is:

## (B) Is the Bible hostile to the Blessed Virgin Mary? Why are some religious groups against her?

The Bible does not say any evil thing about the blessed Mother; rather, she is presented to us as one who kept the faith and treasured the Word of God in her heart (a living example for us – see Lk. 1:45; 11:27-28). In this case, one can say that the Blessed Virgin of Nazareth is truly the Mother of Jesus, for the Bible teaches us that:

"My Mother and brothers are those who hear the Word of God and obey it" (Lk. 8:21; 11:28).

The Blessed Virgin is the only one who could say without troubled conscience: "Yes I kept the Word of God". But with all the passages of the Bible in support of her unique virtues, there are still many people who go around insulting her person and her relationship with her Son, Jesus. Those who talk about the Blessed Mother of Jesus insultingly do not have Bible support for their actions. If the Blessed Virgin Mary were not the Mother of Jesus, would anyone still have the right to insult her? Of course, the answer is: No. We have to learn how to speak with respect. Imagine St. Michael the Archangel: "In his quarrel with the Devil, ... Michael did not dare condemn the Devil with insulting words" (Jude 1:8-11) but we see some religious fanatics attack with insults anything Catholic that they do not understand. What amazes one here is that the Devil who deserves insult is not even insulted by St. Michael, yet man opens his mouth to insult the glorious Mother of Jesus. It is very clear that it is the evil Spirit and not the Spirit of Jesus that speaks through the lips of those who insult the Blessed Mother of our Redeemer. How can the Spirit of Jesus make the following statement about the Blessed Mother:

"And that is why I could implore the dead Mary to pray for me". It is very clear that the guy who wrote this to me is speaking under the rule and guide of the evil spirit. If he were in the light, speaking under the influence of the Spirit of Jesus, Son of Mary, he would never have called the ever glorious Mother of the Saviour of the World, "dead".

A genuine love of Jesus would lead to the love of His Mother; so also a genuine love of the Blessed Mother would naturally move a person to the love of Jesus. If someone were to claim to love Jesus and yet have no regard for the Blessed Mother, we would not need further proof that such a person does not love Jesus.

## Guard yourselves against False Doctrines

We must guard ourselves against false doctrines, for they lead to confusion and sometimes to spiritual death. A case comes to mind here: Having joined a new Christian group that regards themselves as "Saved", a young man severed relationship with his natural family. His reason being that the Christian is commanded by the Bible to love first and foremost, those within the household of faith (Gal. 6:10); others are excluded from the Christian's love and concern. He forgot that the passage of the Scripture which he was referring to counsels us too that "we should do good to everyone" (v. 10). His rejection of his natural family is the result of a dangerous doctrine. What a confusion!

## (C) Are visions, revelations, signs and wonders, proof that a religious sect has the truth?

Some people believe that a true Church can be proved (determined) by the signs and wonders her members perform. In the Catholic Church, we do not look for signs and wonders as a guarantee of holiness and authenticity of our Church. Unfortunately, some of our members go to shop for visions, revelations, prophecies, healings among other religious sects. The result has always been that a good number of such Catholics get lost to those religious groups, while some come back to the Church more confused and spiritually wounded, for one often hears them complaining: "I am confused and worried. I don't know which is the correct thing to believe". Let those who are looking for power – visions, prophecies, healings, that is, those who are anxious to see signs as proof of the presence and power of God, read Mt. 7:21-23 and 2 Th. 2:9-11. The trick of the evil one has always been to charm and deceive people with lies and "wonders" so that they may continue to live in error – Read 1 Kg. 22:19-23. The Bible teaches us that the devil brought Ahab to ruin by causing his prophets to tell him lies. Micaiah said:

"I saw the Lord sitting on his throne in heaven, with all his angels standing beside him. The Lord asked, 'who will deceive Ahab so that he will go and be killed at Ramoth?' Some of the angels said one thing, and others said something else, until a spirit stepped forward, approached the Lord, and said, 'I will deceive him'. 'How?' the Lord asked. The Spirit replied,

'I will go and make all Ahab's prophets tell lies'. The Lord said, 'Go and deceive him. You will succeed'" (1 Kg. 22:19-22).

Ahab had reliable prophets to listen to but he preferred lies to truth and so he got what he loved, lies. God could not force Ahab to accept the truth and hence, He permitted him to be deceived by lying spirits through the lips of false prophets. People who are looking for a religion of convenience (no confession of sins committed, no holy Eucharist etc.) should take note of the consequences of listening to lies and of accepting and committing oneself to doctrines which are contrary to the teaching of the Bible and the teaching authority of the Church (Eph. 3:10; Titus 1:9; 1 Tim. 3:15). The Church, we are told, is the Pillar and support of the Truth.

We must pray to be delivered from wicked teachers and harmful doctrines, for they lead to spiritual death (2 Th 3:2). We are told by the Bible that a time will come when some people will abandon the faith and will "obey lying spirits and follow teachings of demons" (1 Th. 4:1-4). What will they teach? Some will go about teaching people that certain food and drinks are forbidden in Spiritual Life and to support their dangerous doctrines, they will quote the Bible and interpret it to suit their case just in the way some people manipulate the law to serve their interest. Let us ask this question in passing: does the Bible forbid the drinking of any wine? The Bible does not condemn the drinking of wine. It only counsels us to be *moderate* when we drink (Read Rom. 14:14; Col. 2:20-23: Sirach 31:25-31; 32:5-6; Matt. 11:19; 1 Tim. 5:23). In all these passages, we are counselled to drink with sense – moderation. The Bible does not tell us: "Stop drinking wine". And yet some teachers of the Bible continue to teach what Titus 1:10 rightly describes as doctrines that upset many of God's children. We shall come back to this discussion. Meanwhile, let us examine briefly the question of the fate of those who are not baptized into Christ.

### (D) Does the Bible support the view that every unbaptized person is an enemy of God, and therefore will not be saved?

The Catholic Church believes that people who are not baptized *for no fault of their own* can be saved if they are obedient to their conscience. This teaching is contained in the Second Vatican Council's document on the Church. Because of its relevance, I include here the passage of the document that concerns our investigation. Finally, those who have not yet received the gospel are related in various ways to the People of God. In the first place, there are the people to whom the covenants and the promises were given and from whom Christ was born according to the flesh (cf. Rom. 9:4-5). On account of their fathers, these people remain most dear to God, for God does not repent of the gifts He makes nor of the calls He issues (cf. Rom. 11:28-129).

But the plan of salvation also includes those who acknowledge the Creator. In the first place among these are the Moslems, who, professing to hold the faith of Abraham, along with us adore the one and merciful God, who on the last day will judge mankind. Nor is God Himself far distant from those who in shadows and images seek the unknown God, for it is He who gives to all men life and breath and every other gift (cf. Acts 17:25-28), and who as Saviour wills that all men be saved (cf. 1 Tim. 2:4).

*Those also can attain everlasting salvation who through no fault of their own do not know the gospel of Christ or His Church, yet sincerely seek God and, moved by grace, strive by their deeds to do His will as it is known to them through the dictates of conscience. Nor does divine Providence deny the help necessary for salvation to those who without blame on their part, have not yet arrived at an explicit knowledge of God, but who strive to live a good life, thanks to His grace.* Whatever goodness of truth is found among them is looked upon by the Church as a preparation for the gospel. She regards such qualities as given by Him who enlightens all men so that they may finally have life.

But rather often, men, deceived by the Evil One, have become caught up in futile reasoning and have exchanged the truth of God for a lie, serving the creature rather than the Creator (cf. Rom. 1:21, 25). Or some there are who, living and dying in a world without God, are subject to utter hopelessness. Consequently, to promote the glory of God and procure the salvation of all such men, and mindful of the command of the Lord, "preach the gospel to every creature" (Mk. 16:14), the Church painstakingly fosters her missionary work" (The Church, Ch. 2. 16-17).

In Nigeria, one often hears the question: "Will a non-Christian be saved?" Some people ask this question because the Bible says that one has to be baptized before one enters into the kingdom of God (Jn. 3:5-6). Our own question is: Where was the good thief baptized? (Lk. 23:43). We don't know how God will save those who are not baptized. Is His hand short to Save? (Number 11:23).

Now concerning the Christian's relationship to the non-Christians, we know the teaching of the Bible about this. The Bible asks: "What does a believer have in common with an unbeliever?" (2 Cor. 6:14-18). The Bible is referring here to the unbeliever's ungodly ways of life. A Christian is not to have anything to do with such ways but the unbaptized person remains a child of God in need of the new life which comes through Jesus Christ. We have stated how it will be possible for them to be saved.

It is an error therefore to suppose that those who are not baptized are enemies of God. We learn from the Holy Bible that Cornelius, a captain in the Roman Regiment, was a good man, who worshipped God and was highly respected by the people; he was known to be all these (a man of God) even when he had not been baptized. One day, an angel of the Lord appeared to him to announce to him God's new favour. He received the favour of the Holy Spirit before he was baptized into Christ (Acts 10:1-48). If any Christian had, in his myopia, called Cornelius an unbeliever before his baptism, the angels of God would have been laughing the person to scorn. The Bible says: "The Lord knows those who are his" (2 Tim. 2:19).

The sort of 'Christian doctrine' which tells people to disregard those who do not share the same faith with us is atrocious. Some religious sects even reject their blood relations on account of their faith in Christ. What does the Bible teach us?

"If anyone does not take care of his relatives, especially the members of his own family, he has denied the faith and is worse than an unbeliever" (1 Tm. 5:8).

Think of those who despise others, regarding them as unsaved; it is clear from the Bible (looking at the incident of two men who went to the temple to pray) (Lk. 18:9-14) that such an attitude is spiritual pride, and pride is so displeasing to the Lord (James 4:6). People who claim to be righteous should think twice (Lk. 16:15).

Having introduced some of the questions that the present edition of this book will examine, we will now proceed to make a detailed study of the various questions asked.

# Q. 30 Has the Bible anything to say about visions and revelations which some people claim to have?
**(Read 2 Maccabees 15:6-16. God can use visions to encourage us to trust and love Him.**

(1) Abraham had a vision of the angels of the Lord (Gen. 18:1-2).
(2) Moses had a vision of God (Ex. 3:1-22) and described his experience as "strange".
(3) Isaiah, the theologian of God's holiness, saw a vision of the Lord on his throne and Isaiah was almost paralyzed with wonder: "There is no hope for me! I am doomed ... with

my own eyes I have seen the King, the Lord Almight" (Is. 6:1-5).

(4) Tobit 12:12-22 tells us the story of Tobit's vision of Angel Raphael.

(5) Daniel 10:1-21 describes Daniel's vision of an angel. It was an experience of the sublime.

(6) St. Paul talks about Jesus' appearance to over 500 followers at once (1 Cor. 15:1-7).

(7) The Bible contains accounts of visions and dreams, and after the ascension of Jesus, we still hear and read of people who claim to have had visions and revelations. St. Paul was one of such people (2 Cor. 12:1-10).

(8) Catholicism does not teach that visions are to be sought or that when had by anybody, such visions should be disregarded. The Church always discerns carefully in order to know the true visions, realizing that "Even Satan can disguise himself to look like an angel of light" (2 Cor. 11:14). St. Paul teaches us that our life is "a matter of Faith and not of Sight" (2 Cor. 5:7).

(9) It is to be noted that the Bible believes that there are false visions and prophecies but the Lord promised His people in the old: "there will be no more false visions and misleading prophecies" (Ezk. 12:24).

(10) The question however is: are there reasons why God grants visions to some of His children? St. Theresa of Avila explains to us.

(11) God knows that there are souls who, by means of His favours, He can gain for Himself. When His majesty sees that they are in a fair way to be lost, He does not wish that the responsibility shall rest with Him. Though they are in a bad way, and devoid of virtue, He gives them joy, delights and tenderness, which begin to stir their desires, and sometimes, He even raises them to a slight degree of contemplation of short duration. He acts in this way, as I have said, in order to prove whether with the aid of such favours, they will consent to prepare themselves to enjoy Him more often (Theresa: The way of perfection, ch. XVIII).

(12) St. Theresa also explains how it is possible that God may give a dissipated soul an exalted vision and for what reason. "A vision, even a very exalted vision, may be granted by the Lord to a person in an evil way, in order to turn him to Himself, but to raise him to contemplation, that I cannot believe. For that is divine union, in which the Lord regales Himself with the soul and the soul with Him. But the impure soul has no means of delighting in heavenly purity,

nor can the joy of the angels rejoice in a thing that is not His own".

Put in another way, "sometimes God wills to show great favour to persons who are in a bad state, so as to rescue them, by this means, from the hands of the devil" (St. Theresa – The Way of Perfection p. 76 ch. XVIII).

(13) We should be careful of false visions because the devil, as the Bible acknowledges, can come to us in the disguise of a heavenly messenger to murmur dangerous messages into our ears. In all visions and revelations, we must call on the Church to guide us.

(14) In the dialogue of St. Catherine of Siena, we also read how the devil comes to deceive God's children and how we can discern visions. The Eternal Father said to St. Catherine:

"After this, they are often deluded in yet another way by the devil, when he takes on the appearance of light. For the devil gives whatever he sees the mind disposed to desire and receive. So when he sees the mind gluttonous, with its desire set only on spiritual visions and consolations (whereas the soul should set her desire not on these but only on virtue, counting herself unworthy of the other or of receiving affection in such consolations), then, I say, the devil presents himself to that mind under the appearance of light. He does this in different ways; now as an angel, now under the guise of my Truth, now as one or the other of my saints. And this he does to catch the soul with the the book of that very spiritual pleasure she has sought in visions and spiritual delight. And unless she rouses herself with true humility, scorning all pleasure, she will be caught on this hook in the devil's hands. But let her humbly disdain pleasure and cling to love not for the gift but for me, the giver. For, the Devil for all his pride, cannot tolerate a humble spirit".

And should you ask me how one can know that the visitation is from the devil and not from me, I would answer you that this is the sign: If it is the devil who has come to visit the mind under the guise of light, the soul experiences gladness at his coming. But the longer he stays, the more gladness gives way to weariness and darkness and pricking as the mind becomes clouded over by his presence within. But when the soul is truly visited by me, eternal Truth, she experiences holy fear at the first encounter. And with this fear comes gladness and security, along with a gentle prudence that does not doubt even while it doubts, but through self-knowledge considers itself unworthy. So the soul says, "I am not worthy to receive your visitation – but how can I be worthy?" Then she turns to the greatness of my charity, knowing and seeing that I can grant it. For I look not to her unworthiness but to my worth, and so make her worthy to receive me. For I do not scorn the longing with which she calls to me. (Dialogue No. 71, p. 133).

# Q. 31 What does it mean to be born again?

(1) When some people say that they are "born again", others say that they are "transformed" or "renewed". All of them are saying the same thing. The Bible teaches us that anyone joined to Christ is a new creation. "The old order has passed away; now all is new" (2 Cor. 5:17). A person is joined to Christ (incorporated into Him) by baptism (Jn. 3:1-8 – new birth). The Bible tells us to put fleshy desires to death "and put on a new man who grows in knowledge as he is formed anew in the image of his Creator" (Col. 3:5-10). The lives of Zacchaeus (Lk. 19:1-10) and St. Paul, the apostle to the gentiles, illustrate what it means to be "born again". Both of them renounced their old evil way of life – Paul was a persecutor of Christians while Zacchaeus cheated people in order to make himself rich. The Bible teaches us that the two persons changed for good when they met Jesus.

(2) The Bible teaches us too that when we were baptized, we were "born again".

"I am telling you the truth", replied Jesus, "that no one can enter the Kingdom of God unless he is born of water and the Spirit. A person is born physically of human parents, but he is born spiritually of the Spirit" (Jn. 3:3-6).

(3) As the Bible says: we have died to sin and are now alive in Christ Jesus (Romans 6:3-11). This is is what is called "rebirth" or "being born again". In a clear and beautiful way, Paul puts it this way: "When anyone is joined to Christ, he is a new being; the old is gone, the new has come" (2 Cor. 5:17).

(4) To be born again (transformed or changed into a new person) means to be dead to sin; to say goodbye to an old way of living. It means to live in fellowship with Christ Jesus; to become like Him (Rom. 6:11-14; 8:29). Paul was an example of such a person who was changed. He was able to say of himself:

"I have been crucified with Christ,

And the life I now live is not my own;

Christ is living in me. I still live
my life but it is a life of faith in the
Son of God, who loved me and gave himself
for me. I will not treat God's gracious
gift as pointless" (Gal. 2:19-21).

Take note of this: Growth in the Spirit (Christian maturity) is a long and painful process. This transformation is not something magical. It is gradual, effective, but imperceptible (Matt. 17:20-25).

(5) The Bible says:
"All of us, gazing on the Lord's glory with unveiled faces are being transformed from glory to glory into his very image by the Lord who is the Spirit (2 Cor. 3:17-18).

Some people have understood this rebirth or "being born again" to mean, a personal acceptance of Jesus; and so for such people, there are Christians who are not "born again". But the truth is: Anyone who is baptized is "born again", he has received the new life through being joined to Christ in baptism (Romans 6:23; Jn. 3:6). The Bible uses different words for this rebirth: "new creature" (2 Cor. 5:17); a "new man" (Eph. 2:15), a member of the one Body animated (given life) by the one Spirit (1 Cor. 12:13; Eph. 4.4ff), "New life" (Col. 2:13).

(6) Jesus brought us the fullness of life (Jn. 10:10) and He himself said that through the waters of baptism and the gift of the Holy Spirit, this new life will be given (Jn. 3:3, 5). To be "born again", Jesus does not say that one has to be of a particular age. Whoever that is born into this world therefore needs the new life; he or she needs salvation in spite of his or her age (Rom. 6:3-4; 23; 1 Pt. 3:21; 2 Cor. 5:17) – See Question 19 (a).

(7) Kathryn Khulman says: "A man might well trust the Lord and His promise that some day, he would be saved and that some day, he would accept Christ in the forgiveness of his sins: he might well trust the Lord sufficiently to believe that God had the ability to forgive his sins. But it is only if this man possesses an active, power-filled faith for salvation, that he can be "born again" (I Believe in Miracles, p. 202).

(8) Perhaps this is true for adults, but children are born again through baptism as a pure gift of God even though they are not mature enough to make an act of faith. They are children spiritually as well as physically but they are truly alive with the new life that Jesus has given them through the gift of baptism.

(9) We must bear in mind that though baptism has destroyed sin in man, as long as his body has not been "clothed with

immortality" (1 Cor. 15:54), sin can still find a way to reassert itself in a "mortal body" (Jerusalem Bible on Romans 6). Our experience is that the grace of baptism does not guarantee that old bad habits will be done away with immediately without any effort on the part of the "born again child". As soon as a person is freed from sin, he has to relearn how to live his new life according to the Christ he has received. In other words, we have to grow in love – "bear fruit" (Jn. 15:16).

(10) Undoubtedly, God has saved us through the baptism of "new birth" (Titus 3:5-7). And His deeds are wondrous and sincere. Paul told the Christians in Thessalonia: "It is God's will that you grow in holiness" (1 Thes. 4:3). What does this tell us? Just as no child becomes a man on the day he is born, so also we do not reach the full stature of Christ immediately after baptism or after any renewal in the Spirit. This newness in Christ is a process – it is becoming more and more like Christ in our thoughts, words and deeds. It means living under God's grace – the Holy Spirit. Having received this grace, we should not go to sleep. We are not yet face to face with God. We must press on.

(11) We have to be vigilant and prayerfully walk in the Spirit (Gal. 5:16-17). We read in the Bible that Paul realized that he was not yet perfect but that he had to press on (push on towards the glorious end) (Phil 3:12)).

Transformation is an ongoing process. As you grow, you might experience certain changes in some areas of your life. A friend I met at Akatta (Orlu) during my itinerant preaching in 1981, told me how he cried to God about his unchaste life. He was guilty of sin of impurity. After that cry, the Lord rushed into his life and set him free. Since then, he lost the desire for sex. It all seems like a dream to him now. Although he is freed in that area, that does not mean that he is now a saint. One may be chaste but still may not be humble.

(12) So to be totally new in the Lord means much. It means turning over one's whole life to the Lord; living no longer for oneself but for the Lord. One has to yield to the transforming power of the Spirit living in one.

(13) Biblical mystics and prophets were good examples of people who lived in close union with God. The power of God was active in their lives. If one were to talk about spiritual 'giants' they deserve that name. But despite this divine power active in them, these holy women and men of the past were still afraid and distressed, and often times complained. Consider the lives of Elijah and Moses, men

of amazing Spiritual Powers (Sirach 18:1-5; Ex. 17:11-13; Dt. 34:10-12); they experienced human weakness and complained (1 Kg. 19:1-5; Ex. 5:22-23). We have also something to learn in the life of St. Peter, the Apostle. None of us is more directly and immediately in touch with Jesus than this great leader of the College of Apostles. He was a fisherman who denied Jesus even with a curse (Mk. 14:71). But after the Lord had given him the Holy Spirit at Pentecost (Acts 2:1-41), the unlearned, impetuous fisherman became a different man as the Bible testifies:

"The Members of the Council were amazed to see how bold Peter and John were and to learn that they were ordinary men of no education. They realized then that they had been companions of Jesus. But there was nothing that they could say, because they saw the man who had been healed standing there with Peter and John. ... they started discussing among themselves. "What shall we do with these men?" they asked. "Everyone in Jerusalem knows that this extraordinary miracle has been performed by them, and we cannot deny it" (Acts 4:13-20).

(14) Here, we see the case of persons who showed the signs that they have been "born again". The power of the Lord was active in their lives. That was a clear example of rebirth in the Lord.

(15) But did Peter behave differently again – did he, after this, show any sign of one who was not "born again"? The Bible says that on one occasion, the "born again" Peter went wrong. Paul, the Apostle accused him of insincerity, of not being straight-forward in his dealing. The Bible says:

"When Peter came to Antioch, I opposed him in public, because *he was clearly wrong*. Before some men who had been sent by James arrived there, Peter had been eating with the Gentile brothers. But after these men arrived, he drew back and would not eat with them, because he was afraid of those who were in favour of circumcising the Gentiles. The other Jewish brothers started acting like cowards, along with Peter; and even Barnabas was swept along not walking a straight path in line with the truth of the gospel. I said to Peter, in front of them all, "You are a Jew, yet you have been living like a Gentile, not like a Jew. How, then, can you try to force Gentiles to live like Jews?" (Galatian 2:11-14).

Why did Peter act in the way he did? Perhaps his power was waning, which is not true. The truth was: Peter did not become incapable of doing something morally wrong after Pentecost. He was still subject to trials, temptations and faults. Peter had to grow in the Lord. He did not become wholly perfect when the Holy Spirit came on him at the Upper room in the City of Jerusalem.

(16) We feel sad if we do not grow in the Spirit. We have to take courage and struggle on. Although we are weak, the Spirit of the living God will come to our help; He will pray to God within us (Rom. 8:26-30). It is not by our might and strength that we can be changed; we are changed by the Lord's redeeming and glorifying love.

(17) The will of God is that we become holy (transformed). We should co-operate with Him. We are like soldiers on a battlefield; eager to win the battle in which we are engaged, but for a fight to be won, the soldiers have to train, put into practice what they learnt; then victory will be won. Perfection calls for hard work and vigilance. Holiness is a decision. Until we reach heaven, no one can say: "I am all right now". The contest is not over. The winner's crown is for those who have kept the rules (2 Tim. 2:6).

(18) Let those who claim to be born again and are therefore without sin think seriously about the cautious statement of St. Paul, the preacher of grace. St. Paul says:

"My conscience is clear, but that does not mean that I am really innocent. The Lord is the one who passes judgment on me" (1 Cor. 4:4-5).

We have no right to declare ourselves "acquitted", "saved" before the final judgement.

To be born again means that one has got a new heart which is a gift from the Holy Spirit (Ezk. 36:25-27). What sort of heart? It is "a heart which is PURE and without fault, a heart free from evil, malice and shame. Whenever the soul hates sin, and makes itself ready with all its power for the way of virtue, and in conversion of life receives the grace of the Spirit into it, it has become wholly new, it has been created afresh" (St. Gregory of Nyssa, Brev. III, p. 605). St. Paul describes it as complete renewal (Eph. 4:22-24); the putting off of the Old Self with its habits and putting on the New Self (Col. 3:9-10).

*Who knows his own inward state?*

"Do not think of yourself more highly . . . be modest in your thinking" (Rom. 12:3).

(1) "The Lord knows those who are his" (2 Tim. 2:19).

(2) I am not yet perfect (St. Paul) (Phil. 3:12).

(3) "No one can see his own errors; deliver me, Lord, from hidden faults" (Ps. 19:12-13).

(4) 1 Jn. 1:8 teaches that in all mortals are found defects. We are never wholly innocent.

## Q. 32 What does the Bible say about devotion to the saints?

**They pray for us (Jeremiah 15:1; 2 Maccabees 12:43-45; Tobit 12:12; Rev. 5:8)**

(1) Who is a saint? A Saint is a person who loves God and God's children, hence he could be called a godly person (Sirach 44:1ff; Jn. 13:10-11), or "a friend of God" (James 2:23). A Saint is rightly a *champion of faith* in the Lord.

(2) Note that when we talk about the Saints, we do not mean only those in the Bible (Abraham, Moses, Elijah, Peter, Paul, etc.). God does not limit the gift of holiness to those of Bible times. After the resurrection and the writing of the Bible, the Holy Spirit has been raising saints in the Church. The Catholic Church believes this, hence she canonizes some of her children. Anybody who does not agree with the Church should be prepared to say that the Holy Spirit stopped work of transforming people's lives after the writing of the Bible.

(3) Through prayer, preaching and virtuous (excellent) life, the saint makes the world sensitive to the reality and saving love of God.

(4) We should include the saints among our friends. They are exemplary children of God. Making them friends will make a difference in our lives. We are even counselled by the Bible to: *"Remember your former leaders, who spoke God's Message to you. Think back on how they lived and died, and imitate their faith"* (Heb. 13:7). Remember – think of – imitate them, that is the teaching of sacred scripture.

(5) So many Christians have gone ahead of us. They have won the victory and are now with the Lord in glory. In other words, they are alive in the Lord of the living (Matt. 22:31-32). They have something to teach us. We are counselled by the Bible to consider how their lives ended. This is the first lesson we are to learn in the devotion to the saints.

(6) Think about Paul. Even while he was alive on earth, the Apostle advised the Philippian Christians: "keep on imitating me, my brothers, pay attention to those who follow the right example that we have set for you" (Phil. 3:17). And again to the Corinthians, he wrote: "Imitate me, then, just as I imitate Christ" (1 Cor. 11:1).

(7) The Saints are models: people we should look at and learn how to live. In the passages of the Bible quoted, we see Paul the apostle putting himself forward as a model just in the way the Church puts forward Saint Dominic Guzman, St.

Catherine of Siena and other saints as models for us. Remember what Heb. 13:7 says – "consider their lives and imitate their faith".

(8) Unless one is prepared to challenge the Bible, that it is no longer the work of the Holy Spirit, devotion to the saints is in accord with the mind of God, for the Bible says that the saints are alive in the Lord and that we should reflect on the way they lived. Catholic Christians talk to them (prayer). This talking to the saints makes some people angry but if the saints are alive, then one can talk to them.

(9) Judith Tyding in her "Gathering a People" said: "Think of how many books have been published recently on nutrition and good eating habits and how avidly they are read by so many people. We should just as eagerly read the advice of saints on how to maintain and increase spiritual health. Customs may change but spiritual biology remains pretty much the same" (p. 102). Continuing her reflection on the saints, Judith says: "We praise the Lord for the immense variety of the saints who shine like gems in his crown. We honour the saints for their cooperation with grace and their yieldness to the spirit" (p. 142). All these are, of course, the reasons why we invite you to consider the life of the saints – the Bible says we should.

(10) Men and women who have displayed goodness (virtue) on a grand scale, have powerful educative influence on those who read the story of their lives. What is said here is not restricted to the Catholic religion. In other religious traditions, most effective guidance in personal difficulties is given by the lives of model heroes of old. Christian saints are heroes of faith. And we will go to them to learn from their experiences. The Bible counsels us: "If you are willing to listen, you will learn and become wise ... don't miss anything that shows insight. If you find a man with understanding, get up early to call on him; wear out his doorstep with your visits" (Sirach 6:33-35).

(11) We are told by Vatican II that "we seek from the saints example in their way of life, fellowship in their communion, and the help of their intercession" (the Church Ch. 7). It is this role of intercession (our belief that they can and do pray for us) that is very much observed in the Catholics' devotion to the saints. The question is: can the saints in glory (in heaven) pray for us? I have dealt with this question in Question 6. Let us consider the issue once again.

(12) *The Saints have power to Pray for Us*

There is an implicit assumption in the above statement:

(i) It means that one believes with the Church that for God's "faithful people, life is changed, not ended. When the body of our earthly dwelling lies in death, we gain an everlasting dwelling place in heaven". This faith of the Church is the teaching of the sacred Scripture:

(ii) The Bible believes that we shall not be wiped out of existence. We shall continue to live forever after our earthly life (1 Th. 5:1-10; 2 Th. 2:13-14; Phil. 3:11-21; 2 Tm. 1:10; Jn. 11:17-26).

(iii) While in this life, the saints were given certain spiritual powers through the Holy Spirit (Lk. 24:49; Lk. 10:9, Mk. 16:15-18; 1 Cor. 12:4-11). It does not seem to be consistent with the character of God to suppose that He took such powers from them at their death. The Sovereign Lord said to Isaac: "I am the God of your Father Abraham. . . . I will bless you and give you many descendants because of my promise to my servant Abraham" (Gn. 26:24). St. Paul teaches us that God does not withdraw his favours – "the gracious gifts of God and his calling are irrevocable" (Rom. 11:29). We are told that St. Dominic believed that he would be more helpful to us Dominicans after his death than while he was here on earth. He held this view because he believed that when man once enters into the presence of God (heaven), he could exercise greater influence on those on earth. Death does not cut us away from the saints. Death does not rob us of the power which the Holy Spirit deposited in us. In fact, having escaped so many human limitations through death, we receive more powers to do good to those whom we have left behind on earth.

(iv) Think about this: "We ask the prayers of our fellow men even though we know that we could pray directly to God".

If we can ask for prayers from one another, why can't we ask the saints to pray for us? A great charismatic like Paul asks for prayers (see Eph. 6:18-20; Col. 4:2-4). Don't we profess union with them in the Creed? They have triumphed. We are in struggle. How can we be in union with them and not ask them to help us in our struggles?

(v) "When we ask the saints on earth to pray for us, we don't lessen our union with Jesus: neither do we lessen it when we ask the saints in heaven to pray for us. In both cases, we increase our union with him as we unite ourselves with members of his body in prayer. Scripture teaches that God responds when two or more of us agree in prayer with the "great clouds of witnesses" (Heb. 12:1) who are with the Lord. They encouraged and edified us by the witness of their lives on earth and in heaven they intercede with us and for us through Jesus who is "our one mediator between God and men" (WJB, USA Catholic Charismatic N.S.C. Newsletter, May, 1983).

(13) We should love the saints and have the attitude of the Church towards them. St. Theresa of the Little Flower says: "I often pray to the saints without being heard, but the more deaf they appear to be, the more I love them. I do not desire to see either God or the saints, but to rest in this dark night of faith" (John Beevers, *Storm of Glory*, p. 166). I love the saints, for I see God's power shining out in their lives. The Bible sees their wonderful lives as the revelation of the glory of God in history and invites us to praise them (Sirach 44:1-18).

Bible readings: Jer. 15:1; 2 Maccabees 15:12-14; Rev. 5:8; 8:3; 7:4-10; Ex. 32:13-14; Rom. 15:30; Eph. 6:19; Col. 4:3; 1 Th. 5:25; 2 Th. 3:1; Heb. 13:18).

(14) Moses teaches us by his own prayer life that we can appeal to God for His mercy and goodness through His saints; for in Ex. 32:13-14, we see Moses telling God: "Stop being angry; change Your mind ... Remember Your Servants Abraham, Isaac, and Jacob ... So the Lord changed his mind".

# Q. 33 (a) Was the Sabbath a day of rest for Jesus?

(1) The observation of the Sabbath as a day of rest (Ex. 20:8-11), is a religious duty imposed by God on His people, Israel. The Lord said to them "the Seventh day is a day of rest dedicated to me. On that day, no one is to work" (Ex. 20:10-11). God made the world in six days and on the seventh day, He rested from His labour; then He set the Seventh Day as a day of rest (Gen. 2:1-3; 2:3).

(2) The Sabbath was a day of peace, light; a day of rest even for God (Ex. 20:11). It was a day one was forbidden to do any kind of work.

(3) The Sabbath was given to Israel as a sign so that they might know that He has Sanctified them (Ez. 20:12). But the need for rest was more pronounced in the law of the Sabbath.

(i) It was forbidden to light a fire (Ex. 35:3).

(ii) It was forbidden to gather wood (Number 15:32ff).

(iii) It was forbidden to prepare food (Ex. 16:23).

(4) We see the strict observance of this in 1 Maccabees 2:32-38 and Jn. 5:8-16. Anyone who violated the Sabbath was put to death (Lev. 23:3; Num. 15:36; 28:9). The Prophets preached the observance of the Sabbath (Jer. 17:27; Neh. 10:31; 13:15-22). All these show how important the Sabbath was for the Jews.

(5) But Jesus came to the scene of this strict religious observance of the Sabbath and said:

"The Sabbath was made for the good of man; man was not made for the Sabbath" (Mk. 2:27).

And he worked on the Sabbath (Lk. 6:6-11; 13:10-17) and the Synogue official protested that the sick should not be healed on the Sabbath (See also Lk. 14:1ff). Jesus' argument was that just as His Father works, so He too must be working (Jn. 5:17). The Jews got angry with Jesus for saying this because they believed that only God could work on the Sabbath. Why? God should work because he has to create and preserve life and that of course, means continuous work on His part. So when Jesus said that He had to be working because His Father, God, was working, He was claiming equality with God. The reaction of the Jews was clear: They were determined to kill Him (Jn. 5:18).

# Q. 33 (b) Is Saturday or Sunday the Sabbath day?

## Sunday replaces Saturday – (Saturday was the Old Testament Sabbath day)

From the evidence in the New Testament, the first day of the week, Sunday, became a day of worship and preaching the gospel and organizing almsgiving.

(1) "Now, concerning what you wrote about the money to be raised to help God's people in Judea, You must do what I told the Churches in Galatia to do. Every Sunday, each of you must put aside some money, in proportion to what he has earned ..." (1 Cor. 16:1-2).

(2) For St. John, Sunday was the "Lord's day" (Rev. 1:10).

(3) On the first day of the week (Sunday) the early Christians broke the bread (fellowship meal – Acts 20:7).

Jesus did not cancel the Sabbath but He didn't put it on the same level that some Christians put it today. We must see things in the way he saw it; that is what makes a good disciple. Jesus says that He has power over the Sabbath (Mk. 2:28) and hence the complaints against him (Jn. 5:16-17).

(4) For Jesus, the apostles and the early Church as a whole, the most important day was Sunday (Jn. 20:1-22), the day Jesus rose from the dead. It was the first day of the week, a day of worship (Acts 20:7; 1 Cor. 16:2; Rev. 1:10) and of joy. According to St. John, on that day, the "disciples were filled with joy at seeing the Lord" (Jn. 20:20-21). It was a day of new mission: "As the Father sent me, so I send you" (v. 21). And then of course, they received the highest gift from above, viz the Holy Spirit (v. 22). This is why Sunday is greater than Saturday and the emphasis shifted from Saturday (Old Testament Sabbath observance) to Sunday observance as a day of rest, of peace, of joy, of hope of eternal life; *Saturday did not reveal eternal life to us, Sunday did.* The Jews of the present day still venerate Saturday because they do not believe in the resurrection of Jesus which ushered in a new Creation – God did something extraordinarily new on Sunday.

(5) The early Christians did not take Saturday as very important. Those who still think that Saturday is the real day of worship are practising Old Testament Religion. Jesus, by his resurrection on Sunday, has made Sunday a day of hope, glory, praise, thanksgiving; in short, a day of worship.

(6) Sunday points to what is to come – a life of thankfulness and joy. It is the promise of God. We shall celebrate. We shall rest – eternal sabbath, eternal rest in God (Is. 25:6-9; Rev. 14:13).

(7) Heb. 4:1-11 teaches us the deeper meaning of the Sabbath rest. We are promised eternal Sabbath:

"Now, God has offered us the promise that we may receive that rest he spoke about. Let us take care, then, that none of you will be found to have failed to receive that promised rest. For we have heard the Good News, just as they did. They heard the message, but it did them no good, because when they heard it, they did not accept it with faith. We who believe, then, do receive that rest which God promised. It is just as he said:

"I was angry and made a solemn promise:
'They will never enter the land where I would have given them rest'!

He said this even though his work had been finished from the time he created the world. For somewhere in the

53

Scriptures, this is said about the seventh day: "God rested on the seventh day from all his work".

This same matter is spoken of again: "They will never enter that land where I would have given them rest". Those who first heard the Good News did not receive that rest, because they did not believe. There are, then, others who are allowed to receive it. This is shown by the fact that God sets another day, which is called "Today". Many years later he spoke of it through David in the scripture already quoted:

"If you hear God's voice today, do not be stubborn". If Joshua had given the people the rest that God had promised, God would not have spoken later about another day. As it is, however, there still remains for God's people a rest like God's resting on the seventh day. For whoever receives that rest which God promised will rest from his own work, just as God rested from His. Let us, then, do our best to receive that rest, so that no one of us will fail as they did because of their lack of faith" (Heb. 4:1-11).

(8) St. Augustine observes that in the eternal felicity of God, in its perpetual sabbath, "we shall sing the mercies of the Lord for all eternity".

(9) The greatest of Sabbaths is the eternal vision of God. St. Augustine says:

"The psalm says, 'sing the mercies of the Lord for all eternity'? Nothing will give more joy to that City than this song to the glory of the grace of Christ by whose blood we have been set free. There that precept will find fulfilment: 'Be still, and know that I am God'. That will truly be the greatest of Sabbaths; a Sabbath that has no evening, the Sabbath that the Lord approved at the beginning of creation, where it says, 'God rested on the seventh day from all his works, which he had been doing; and *God blessed the seventh day* and made it holy, because on that day he rested from all his works, which God had begun to do'.

We ourselves shall become that seventh day, when we have been replenished and restored by his blessing and sanctification. There we shall have leisure to be still, and we shall see that he is God, whereas we wished to be that ourselves when we fell away from him, after listening to the Seducer saying: 'You will be like gods'. Then we abandoned the true God, by whose creative help we should have become gods, but by participating in him, not by deserting him. For what have we done without him? We have 'fallen away in his anger'. But now restored by him and perfected by his greater grace, we shall be still and at leisure for eternity, seeing that he is God, and being filled by him when he will be all in all.

For all our good works, when they are understood as being his works, not ours, are then reckoned to us for the attainment of that Sabbath rest. If we ascribe them to ourselves, they will be 'servile work', and it said that, on the Sabbath, 'You shall do no servile work'. I gave them my Sabbaths as a sign between me and them; so that they might know that I am the Lord, and that I sanctify them.

"After this present age God will rest, as it were, on the seventh day, and he will cause us, who are the seventh day to find our rest in him".

However, it would be a long task, to go on to discuss each of those epochs in detail. The important thing is that the seventh day will be our Sabbath, whose end will not be an evening, but the Lord's Day an eighth day, as it were, which is to last forever, a day consecrated by the resurrection of Christ, foreshadowing the eternal rest not only of the spirit but of the body also. There we shall be still and see; we shall see and we shall love; we shall love and we shall praise. Behold what will be, in the end, without end! For what is our end but to reach that kingdom which has no end? (City of God, BK XXII, Ch. 30).

# Q. 34 Can a Christian join the army, police and the law profession?

(1) The Bible does not condemn any of these professions. It however, condemns evil practices that members of such professions practise.

(2) When the soldiers came to John the Baptist, he did not condemn them because they were soldiers; he simply gave them advice on how they should live:

"Denounce no one falsely. Be content with your pay" (Lk. 3:14). Acts 10:1-48 proves to us that someone in the Military force can be a good man. Read the passage of the Bible concerned (See also Lk. 7:1-9).

What is said here applies to the study and profession of law. Some people are trained to interpret the law of the state. And the goal of law is the preservation of justice in society. What serves to put order in human affairs, is good. Law is intended to ensure that no one takes advantage over his neighbour. So those who study law and use it to defend the rights of people are doing works of love.

(3) In the trial of Jesus, the law was not allowed to have its course. Pilate told the elders, the Chief priests and teachers of the law that he had examined Jesus but "had not found him guilty of any of the crimes you accuse him of" (Lk. 23:13-25). Pilate wanted to set Jesus free because in his interpretation of the law, Jesus was not guilty of any crime. The law was in favour of Jesus but the Judge took side with the enemies of Christ and the law (Jn. 19:12-14).

(4) We discover that before this time, Nicodemus was already seeking the aid of the law to save Jesus' right to life.

"According to our law, we cannot condemn a man before hearing him and finding out what he has done" (Jn. 7:51).

But some of the Jewish authorities had made up their minds that the law was of no use in their conflict with Jesus. They brushed the law aside by threatening Pilate that they would report him to the Emperor and Pilate handed Jesus over to them to kill. If they had followed the law, Jesus wouldn't have been killed. This is a case of people refusing to do the truth. They know what is right but they refuse to do it. We find that some people do the same in every profession. They know what is right, but they do not often-times do it because it does not serve their interest.

(5) When some people abuse the law, that does not make the law bad. When a lawyer who ought to use the law to protect people's rights and privileges uses the law for his own selfish ends, such an attitude does not make the law profession as a whole an evil. A Christian who enters the law profession should use that profession to do good to God's children – to defend their rights and awaken them to their responsi-bilities. The law does not only defend our rights, it also calls us to do our duties and when we fail to do so, it is the office of the lawyer to call our attention to what the law says we should be doing.

(6) If Jesus was a Roman citizen by law (not even by birth), He would not have been insulted in the way they did him, for it was forbidden by the law to scourge and crucify a Roman Citizen. To scourge a Roman Citizen was a crime punishable by death. In Philippi, police officers were afraid because they beat Paul and Silas, who were Roman Citizens (Acts 16:37-39). So they went and apologised to them. Paul believed in the protection of the law and when the Judge, Ananias, broke the law during Paul's trial, the apostle cursed Ananias.

"God will certainly strike you. You whitewashed wall! You sit there to judge me according to the law, yet you break the law by ordering them to strike me!" (Acts 23:1-4).

Here, St. Paul is not condemning the Judge because he is in the law profession, the judge is condemned because he broke the law. But when Paul met a lawyer, Felix, who knew what the law requires in the case brought against Paul, he "ordered the officer in charge of Paul to keep him under guard, but to give him some freedom and allow his friends to provide for his needs" (Acts 24:22-23). Here, we see a lawyer using law to ensure that Paul enjoys his fundamental right, namely freedom which the law allows.

(7) We may do well to read Acts Chapters 24, 25, 26 where Paul made several appeals to the law in defence of his right to live, and the right to practise his new found faith. At the end of St. Paul's legal battle in Caesarea, the Judge, Agrippa said: "This man could have been released if he had not appealed to the Emperor" (Acts 26:32). The law is meant to ensure that justice is done. Whoever does that sort of job is doing something good.

# Q. 35  Why should we fast?

(1) By fasting, we train our will in order to acquire the virtue of self control when we are faced with objects of pleasure. St. Paul says:

"I harden my body, with blows and bring it under complete control, to keep myself from being disqualified after having called others to the contest" (1 Cor. 9:27).

Fasting is an act of self-discipline and the importance of self-discipline can be seen in the life of a city that is well guarded and defended by vigilant soldiers. A thinker says: "An enemy will not even attempt an attack on those who are really prepared to meet it" (Aristotle's Politics). A city well disciplined and defended is never easily overthrown by an aggressive enemy. What really marks a city is power and effectiveness and no city can attain power and effectiveness if her citizens spend their time eating and drinking and enjoying fruitless conversations and all sorts of fun. There has to be discipline, vigilance, a sense of duty inside the city. An external enemy dare not attack a well-organized city. From this little look at the city, we can see that a life (we are like a little city) that is not well-organized; nor disciplined (ordered) is bad.

To discipline oneself has its blessings. It helps us to stay sober and alert – for we are always surrounded by danger

(1 Pet. 5:8-10). We are by nature, weak. We should not weaken ourselves the more by soft life, rather, we should take all the necessary means to make ourselves strong. What are the means? Mortification of our will, of our tongue, of our appetite and all other desires; the practice of silence, continuous study of sacred scripture, spiritual books and prayer. We should endeavour to do all these whether we find it enjoyable or not.

It is important for us to know however, that merit consists in doing charity and justice (Is. 58:1-9). This is the only way to inner peace – the beginning of salvation.

(3) Fasting is a serious form of self-denial because in it a person gives up the pleasure of eating for a particular time as a religious duty. By it, we develop our moral powers to do good and avoid evil. In short, it helps the will to opt for the good. There are instances in the Old and New Testament times when the Lord's people had to proclaim a fast (Is. 58:3-12; Joel 2:12-13; Lk. 2:37; 4:2; 7:33-34; Mt. 17:21; Mk. 2:18; Acts 13:1-3). Jesus himself did fast for forty days (Lk: 4:1-4), thus leaving us an example that there is need for this kind of spiritual exercise. Although we may not be able to do a forty day fast, we should not brush it aside as an ancient spirituality. We need self-control when we are faced with those things which appeal to our senses.

St. Thomas Aquinas gave three reasons why we fast:

(a) To check the desires of the flesh. So St. Paul says in fasting, in chastity (2 Cor. 6:5), meaning that fasting is a safeguard for chastity. Lust loses its heat through spareness of food and drink.

(b) "That the mind may more freely raise itself to contemplation of the heights. We read in the book of Daniel that it was after a fast of three weeks that he received the revelation from God" (Daniel 10:2-4).

(c) "To make satisfaction for sin. This is the reason given by the prophet Joel, 'Be converted to me with all your heart, in fasting and in weeping' (Joel 2:12). And here is what St. Augustine writes on the matter. "Fasting purifies the soul. It lifts up the mind, and it brings the body into subjection to the spirit. It makes the heart contrite and humble, scatters the clouds of desire, puts out the flames of lust and enkindles the true light of chastity" (Aquinas, *Meditations and Readings for Lent*, p. 48).

(d) In the infant Church, fasting was in practice (Acts 13:1-3).

(5) All these are not to be understood to mean that when once one fasts, that is the end of the conflict between the flesh and the spirit. There is no doubt that those who sincerely undertake to suffer the flesh for the love of god will be rewarded in a way and at a time the Lord Himself decides. It is to be understood however that one can fast and still be uncharitable. The ancient Israel was sometimes guilty of this (Is. 58:3-12). God of course, did not appreciate such fasts. They did not bring blessings to those who did such fasts. It is for this reason that we learn in St. Catherine of Siena's dialogue that "merit consists in the virtue of love alone, flavoured with the light of true discretion, without which the soul is nothing" (Dial. p. 58).

(6) Christian mortality enjoins us to pursue justice and peace. The Lord takes delight in this more than in fasting which makes a person self-centred instead of reaching out in love to God's children.

**Study of Bible passages that deal with Fasting and Mortification**

**FASTING:** Esdra 8:23; 2 Esdra 1:4; Dan. 9:3; Jonas 3;5; Matt. 9:15; Mk. 2:20; 9:28; Lk. 5:35; Acts 13:3; 14:22; 2 Cor. 6:5, 11:27 – Christ's fast Mt. 4:2; Lk. 4:2; Is. 58:3-12; Joel 2:12-13; Lk. 2:37; 4:2; 7:33-34; 18:9-14; Mt. 17:21; Mk. 2: 18; Acts 13:1-3.

**MORTIFICATION:** Mk. 8:34-37;9:43-48;

Love takes Priority:

(1) Micah 6:6-8; Hosea 6:5-6; Tobit 12:7
(2) Lk. 7:47; 10:36-37; 18:18-30; 21:1-4
(3) Lk. 8:19-21; 11:27-28; 1 Jn. 5:2

**Alms-Giving:**

Acts 10:4; 1 Pt. 4:8

# Q. 36 (a) Does the Bible forbid any food or wine?

(1) The Bible teaches us that everything God made is good. Gn. 1:31 says: "God saw all that he had made, and it was very good". Some people condemn some food and some kind of drink and persuade others to reject them as if such things are evil. The Bible calls these the "teachings of demons" which are spread by deceitful liars. The clear statement of the Bible on this matter is precisely this:

"Such people teach that it is wrong to marry and to *eat certain foods*. But God created those foods to be eaten, after a prayer of thanks, by those who are believers and have come to know the truth. Everything that God has created is good; nothing is to be REJECTED, but everything is to be received with a prayer of thanks, because the word of God and the prayer make it acceptable to God" (1 Tm. 4:1-5).

What is said about food here applies to wine or any kind of alcoholic drink. The Bible does not forbid the drinking of wine or any kind of alcoholic drink. God made them and they are "to be received with a prayer of thanks" (1 Tm. 4:4-5).

(3) St. Paul says: "I know on the authority of the Lord Jesus that nothing is unclean in itself; it is only when a man thinks something is unclean that it becomes so for him" (Rom. 14:14). What St. Paul says here is in agreement with the teaching of Jesus. St. Mark says that Jesus declared that all foods are fit to be eaten (Mk. 7:19). God made food and drink and He is pleased with it. Anybody who teaches a different thing is teaching the doctrine of men or those of demons. The Bible asks:

"If with Christ you have died to cosmic forces, why should you be bound by rules that say, "Do not handle! Do not taste! Do not touch! as though you were still living a life bounded by this world? Such prescriptions deal with things that perish in their use. They are based on merely human precepts and doctrines" (Colosians 2:20-23).

(4) It has been said that on account of the influence of wine, Lot was deceived to have sex with his daughters (Genesis 19:30-38). The conclusion most people come to from this incident is: Wine is bad. Whoever argues this way mocks the Bible which tells us that God made everything and found them to be good (Gn. 1:31).

What we must guard against:

(5) In the Spiritual Life, we are counselled to be careful of going to excesses – not to get deeply involved in the pursuit of pleasure which comes from food, drink and sex. The Bible says that such a life is sheer vanity:

(i) "I said in my heart: I will go and abound with delights, and enjoy good things. And I saw that this also was vanity (Ecclesiastes 2:1).

(ii) She who lives in pleasure, is dead while she is living (1 Tim. 5:6).

(6) The Bible does not condemn any kind of alcoholic drink. It however, warns us about the evil in excessive drinking – the abuse of wine (Prov. 23:20:21).

(i) "Don't try to prove your manhood by how much you can drink. Wine has been the ruin of many. An arrogant man's character shows through when he is in a drunken argument, in the same way that iron is tested when it is heated red-hot and then dipped in water. Wine can put new into you if you drink it in *moderation* . . . wine was created to make us happy. If you drink it in *moderation* and at the right time, it can lift your spirits and make you cheerful, but if you drink when you are angry and upset, it leads to headaches, embarrassment, and disgrace" (Sirach 31:25-31; 32:5-6).

(ii) Ps. 104:15 – says that God gave us:
   (i) Wine to make us happy
   (ii) Olive oil to make us cheerful
   (iii) Bread to give us strength.

(iii) Prov. 20:1 says: "Drinking *too much* makes you loud and foolish. It is stupid to get drunk". The blameable act here is getting drunk or drinking too much; it is not an evil to drink, at least the Bible does not say so.

(iv) Prov. 23:29-35 – tells us the evil effect of drinking *too much* – it will make us miserable and pitiable.

As an official guideline, the Bible says that helpers in the Church must not drink "too much wine" (1 Tm. 3:8). It does not say that they should not drink wine at all.

In O.T. food and wine symbolise God's offer of life (Prov. 9:5; Sirach 24:19-21). Wine is not evil, otherwise the Bible would not have mentioned it as a symbol of God's perfect gift – life.

(v) Jesus, the author and finisher of our faith (Heb. 12:2), did not condemn wine: He himself would seem to have taken it. His opponents accused Him of drinking as He himself said:
   "When John came, he fasted and drank no wine, and everyone said, 'He has a demon in Him'! When the Son of man came, he ate and DRANK and everyone said, 'Look at this man! He is a glutton and WINE-DRINKER" (Matt. 11:19).

(7) When St. Paul was enumerating the qualities of a Church leader, he mentioned among other things, that the Church leader must not be a *drunkard*; St. Paul did not say that a Church leader should not drink (1 Tm. 3:2-3).

What we have come to know in the teaching of the Bible can be summarized as follows:

(i) The Bible does not condemn wine nor the drinking of it, for Our Lord teaches us that: "It is not what goes into a person's mouth that makes him ritually unclean; rather, what comes out of it makes him unclean"

(Mt. 15:10; Mk. 7:18-19). St. Mark says that "In saying this, Jesus declared that all foods are fit to be eaten" (Mk. 7:19).

(ii) Following the teaching of Jesus therefore, it is not what goes into a person's mouth (for example, wine) that makes a person unclean, but rather, it is what comes out of a person's heart (evil ideas) that defiles a person. It is true that the Bible says that the ancient Israel lost their sense through *wine*, they were led into prostitution – preferred disgrace to honour (Hosea 4:11 and 18), but this does not mean that wine is bad. Reading the Bible, one does not find where it condemns the drinking of wine as such; however, it condemns *too much* drinking (drunkeness or excessive drinking) of it.

(8) What we have here is basically the teaching of the Bible about wine. Anybody who holds a different view is teaching his own doctrine.

(9) Someone once asked: "How little is little?" This calls for a consideration of what constitutes the mean (the reasonable quantity) we need to drink in order not to offend the right rule. The Bible does not tell us what is the reasonable quantity or what would constitute "too much" when one gets down to drink. For one person, one drink may be too much, but for another person, two drinks may not be too much. The questions about quantity are bound up with the circumstances of the individual case (Aristotle – Nicomachean Ethics, Bk. 2).

(10) Paul, one of the greatest Christian teachers of Faith and Morals, has this to say:

(i) "Avoid getting drunk" (Eph. 5:18). St. Paul does not say: "don't drink". As a matter of fact, he recommended a little wine for the health of Timothy: "Do not drink water only, but take *a little wine* to help your digestion, since you are sick so often" (1 Tm. 5:23).

(11) Everything God made (Wine, Food, Water, Trees, Flowers, Animals, etc.) is good (Gn. 1:1-25). Those who condemn wine or even the drinking of it are telling God that what He Himself made, is an evil; what an attack on God's loving providence! The Bible says:

> "Everything is pure to those who are themselves pure; but nothing is pure to those who are defiled and unbelieving, for their minds and consciences have been defiled" (Titus 1:15). (See Question 20).

## William Barclay's View:

(12) Barclay has this to say on Wine:

> The Old Testament looks on wine as one of the good gifts of God; it nowhere demands total abstinence from it;

but there is no book which is more intensely aware of its dangers, and which more unsparingly condemns its misuse.

Finally, we turn to the evidence of the New Testament. Jesus Himself was not a total abstainer; they could slanderously call him a glutton and a drunkard (Mt. 11:19; Lk. 7:34). The miracle of Cana of Galilee shows Jesus willing to share in the simple joys of a wedding-feast (Jn. 2:1-11). Paul can send advice to Timothy: "No longer drink only water, but use a little wine for the sake of your stomach and your frequent ailments" (1 Timothy 5:23).

But the voice of warning is there. The bad servant in the parable eats and drinks with the drunken (Mt. 24:49). "Do not get drunk with wine", says Paul, "for that is debauchery" (Eph 5:18). When the New Testament lists sins, sins in which the Christians must have no part, revelry, drunkenness, carousing regularly appear among the forbidden things (Rom. 13:13; 1 Corinthians 6:10; Gal. 5:21). There are even times when drunken conduct invades the Church and its Love Feasts (1 Cor. 11:21; 2 Pet. 2:13), and there are those who have to be warned against drunkeness at night (1 Thessalonians 5:7). In particular, those who hold office in the Church are warned against any excess. There must be no association with a drunkard (1 Cor. 5:11). The older women are not to be addicted to drink (Titus 2:3). The deacons are not to be slaves to wine, and the bishop is not to be a drunkard (1 Timothy 3:8; 3:3; Titus 1:7).

One passage must have special treatment. The saying in Colossians 2:21 is often used as evidence for total abstinence.

'Do not handle; do not taste; do not touch'. It is precisely the reverse. In the passage, Paul is dealing with those who are preaching a false asceticism, and who are trying to introduce new food laws which will prohibit people from eating this, that, and the next thing. And this saying is the saying of the heretics, who are trying to mislead the people. It is the heretics and the misguided and misleading teachers who say, 'Do not handle; do not taste; do not touch', and this the Revised Standard Version makes quite clear by putting the sentence into quotation marks, in order to show that it is a quotation from the false teaching of the heretical teachers. This sentence tells us, not what to do, but what not to do.

This, then, is the New Testament evidence. Once again, there is nowhere, any demand for total abstinence, neither in the words nor in the example of Jesus or of his followers, but there is a strong warning against the misuse and the danger of drink. In this case, we have no rule and regulation on which to fall back. We must work out our own conclusion.

(i) The prevalence of the use of alcohol in all grades of society is ample proof of its attraction. It makes entertaining easy; it relaxes tensions and eases the atmosphere of a social occasion. There is the occasional medical use of it, of which even Paul's advice to Timothy is an example. We need not argue about the attraction; it is there.

(ii) But in addition to the attraction, there are obvious dangers.

(a) There is the fact that the effect of alcohol on a man is quite unpredictable. One man may be able to take it in even large quantities with no visible ill effect; another man may have that built into his composition which makes him an alcoholic, and he may be such that any use of alcohol will have the most disasterous effects. None of these effects can be predicted in advance. Only experiment shows how a man will react, and it can be argued that the experiment carries with it such a risk that it is unwise to make it.

(b) There is the danger of excess. It is quite true that the danger of excess arises with any pleasure, and that scripture warns against gluttony just as strongly as it warns against drunkenness. But drunkenness is a specially ugly thing in a drunken person, and a specially unhappy thing for those with whom he lives and who share his life and home.

(c) With alcohol, there arises the question of addiction". (William Barclay, Ethics in a Permissive Society, pp. 136-139).

NOTE: I have quoted extensively from William Barclay to show that our position is supported by such an eminent Bible Scholar.

# Q. 36 (b) When the Bible talks about wine, does it refer to the kind of drink (beer, brandy, whisky and other hot drinks) we have today?

Let us gather facts from the Bible:

(1) Noah drank some wine and became *drunk* and lay naked (Gen. 9:21).

(2) Melchizedek, king of Salem, brought out bread and wine for Abram (Gn. 14:18).

(3) Wine was used for Libation – a fourth of wine (Ex. 29:40, Num. 28:14).

(4) The Israelites sat down to eat and *drink*, and rose up to revel (Ex. 32:6).

(5) Nazirites were to abstain from wine and *strong drink* (Num. 6:3).

(6) Eli, thinking Anna drunk, said, "Sober up from your wine!" (1 Sam. 1:14).

(7) Abigail got 200 loaves and two skins of wine ... as gifts for David (1 Sam. 25:18ff).

(8) David made Uriah drunk (2 Sam. 11:13). Ammon was killed when merry with wine (2 Sam. 13:28ff).

(9) Nehemiah offered wine to the King – and was granted all he asked for (Neh. 2:1ff).

(10) Judith overcame Holofernes drunk with wine (Judith 12:19-20).

(11) Job's trial began while his sons and daughters were eating and drinking wine (Job. 1:13).

(12) Amos condemned the complacent in Zion for drinking wine from bowls (Am. 6:6).

(13) True fasting, according to Zechariah, is not abstaining from food and drinks but consists in true judgment, kindness and compassion (Zec. 7:5ff).

## In the New Testament

(1) People do not pour new wine into old wine skins (Mt. 9:17).

(2) John came not eating nor drinking, you said he is mad – on the other hand, you called the Son of Man a glutton and drunkard (Mt. 11:18-19; Lk. 7:33-34).

(3) He took the cup, gave thanks and gave it to them (Mt. 26:27; Mk. 14:23; Lk. 22:17).

(4) John the Baptist would never drink wine or *strong drink*.

(5) The Samaritan dressed his wounds, pouring in oil and wine (Lk. 10:34).

(6) The waiter tasted the water-made-wine (Jn. 2:9).

(7) The people said at Pentecost: they have had too much new wine (Acts 2:13).

(8) The cup of the Lord (1 Cor. 10:14-22; 11:25-26).

(9) Avoid getting *drunk on wine*; that leads to debauchery (Eph. 5:18).

(10) Paul advised Timothy to take little wine (1 Tim. 5:23).

## Remark:

What wine was in Biblical times is what wine is today. Wine was different from any other alcoholic drinks or strong drinks in Biblical times just as wine is different from beer and strong drinks today. (Thanks to Bro. Anthony Aroboi for some of these ideas).

One point is important to bear in mind and that is: Wine in the Bible had the power to intoxicate those who drank it as we read:

(i) "You are doomed! You get up early in the morning to start drinking, and you spend long evenings getting drunk" (Is. 5:11-12).

(ii) "You are doomed! Heroes of the wine bottle! Brave and fearless when it comes to mixing drinks" (Is. 5:22).

(iii) "Wine, both old and new, is robbing my people of their senses" (Hosea 4:11).

Why was wine in the Biblical times able to do this? It was able to rob people of their senses because it contained some elements of alcohol. What wine did to Bible people, beer or any hot drink could do to *those who drink it in excess.*

Although wine contains some alcohol and could intoxicate as beer or any hot drink does, the Bible still does not condemn wine. It will be wrong therefore to argue that beer or any hot drink is bad simply because, containing a high quantity of some elements of alcohol, it could affect our mental powers.

Some people argue this way:

"Wine hurts some people. Therefore wine is evil". This is fallacious. Can we say: "Motor cars sometimes hurt some people. Therefore, motor cars are evil". This kind of reasoning is ridiculous.

It is wrong to condemn wine or any kind of drink simply because some people make bad use of it.

# Q. 37 What does the Bible say about the use of Holy Water, Holy Oil, Incense, and other blessed objects which the Catholic Church calls Sacramentals?

## 1. WATER:

St. Augustine says:

"Water is just water and nothing else but divine power enters into this simple element, and it becomes a Sacrament".

Put differently, water is what we can see and touch (matter), but when God's power enters into it, the water so touched by God's power, becomes a means by which we receive grace (favour) from God, who is love. This is proved to be true by the Bible in the story of Naaman.

"Naaman was a Syrian who suffered from leprosy, and no one could cleanse him. Then a young captive girl said that there was a prophet in Israel who could cleanse him from his infection. Having taken silver and gold, we are told, he went to the king of Israel. When the latter heard why he had come, he rent his clothes, saying that there was really a plot against him, since demands were being made of him which did not lie in his royal power. Elisha, however, sent word to the king to send the Syrian to him, that he might know there was a God in Israel. And when he had come, he made him bathe seven times in the river Jordan. Then Naaman began to reflect that he had better waters in his own country, in which he had often bathed without ever being cleansed of his leprosy. This held him back, and he was inclined not to obey the command of the prophet. But his servant advised and persuaded him to give way, and he bathed. He was cleansed instantly, and he understood that it is not by water but by grace that a man is cleansed". (2 Kg. 5:1ff. See Roman Breviary III, p. 307). In Jn. 9:6-11 We see Jesus ordering a man born blind to wash in water so as to regain his sight.

## 2. OIL:

Oil was used for healing. Here, we mean Olive Oil. In Esther 2:12, it refers to myrrh, but everywhere else, it refers to olive oil. Olive oil was used for food, similar to the way we use butter (1 Kg. 17:12), a cosmetic (Is. 61:3), a lamp fuel (Ex. 25:6) *and as a healing agent* (Is. 1:6; Mark 6:13). It was used for an ingredient for the meal offering also (Lev. 2:1). Oil was an important object of commerce (Ezek 27:17); After the olives were shaken from the trees (Deut. 24:20; Is. 17:6), they were pressed. (Charles F. Pfeiffer, The New Combined Bible Dictionary, pp 315-316).

## 3. INCENSE:

Incense is an aromatic compound which gives forth its perfume in burning. Instructions for incense for the Jewish altar are found in Ex. 30:22-38. The gold plated altar of incense in the Holy Place was used twice daily (Ex. 30:1-9). On the annual day of atonement, the high priest burnt incense in the Holy of Holies (Lev. 16:12, 13; Lev. 10:1, Is. 1:13; Lk. 19:10; Rev. 8:3) (The New Combined Bible Dictionary, p. 237).

# Q. 38 Is faith in Jesus Christ sufficient for salvation?

**1. FAITH IS NECESSARY BUT NOT SUFFICIENT FOR SALVATION**

It would seem that when once a person puts his faith in Christ (cf. Jn. 6: 29 and 40), he will be saved, for the Bible says: "For if you confess with your lips that Jesus is Lord, and belief in your heart that God raised him from the dead, you will be saved. Faith in the heart leads to justification, confession on the lips to salvation ... Everyone who calls on the name of the Lord will be saved (Rom. 10:9-13).

It is true that "without faith, it is impossible to please God. Anyone who comes to God must believe that He exists and that he rewards those who seek him" (Heb. 11:6). Heb. 11:40 teaches us the blessings of faith. Read 1 Pt. 1:8-9.

(2) What exactly is Faith? The faith which the Bible talks about is not something mental – being aware that God exists. By faith here, the Bible means a firm trust in the saving love of God. It is for this reason that St. John the Evangelist teaches that:

    (i) "For him who believes there will be no judgment" (Jn. 5:24). This loving trust leads to justification (Rom. 10:10).

    (ii) He who believes is already risen (Jn. 11:25f; cf. Jn. 6:40).

    (iii) He who believes walks in the light (Jn. 12:46).

    (iv) He who believes possesses eternal life (Jn. 12:46).

    (v) But "He who does not believe is already condemned" (Jn. 3:18).

    (vi) Faith is victory over the world of sin (1 Jn. 5:4). No one who believes in him will be put to shame" (Rom. 10:11). (Xavier Leon-Dufour. Dict. of Biblical Theology pp. 162-163).

(3) But faith in Jesus calls for believe in and practice of what Jesus taught, for He Himself asks: "Why do you call me, 'Lord, Lord', and don't do what I tell you? Everyone who comes to me, and listens to my words, and obeys them – I will show you what he is like ..." (Lk. 6:46-47). It is doing what we learnt from Christ that makes us His disciples.

"If you live according to my teaching, you are truly my disciples; then you will know the truth, and the truth will set you free" (Jn. 8:31-32).

Jesus teaches us to believe in Him and in His Father (Jn. 14:1); but He also teaches us a new commandment of love (Jn. 13:34; Mk. 12:28-31). The New Testament stresses this virtue of love more than the virtue of faith. And the happiness of the Christian consists not just in faith but in the exercise of love. The Bible says that what matters is Faith which works through love (Gal. 5:6).

"Now that you know this truth, how happy you will be if you put it into practice" (Jn. 13:17).

What truth is Jesus telling us? It is not faith in His Person, but faith-in-action; that is, the practice of love and service. This practice of love and concern for others will bring the followers of Jesus priceless blessing – the Father and the Son will come and dwell with the person (Jn. 14:23).

(4) The Bible also teaches us that not all those who call 'Jesus, Jesus' will be saved (Mt. 7:20-23). As has been pointed out when the Bible talks about faith, it means "faith which expresses itself through love" (Gal. 5:6). The Apostle Paul says:

"There are in the end three things that last: faith, hope, and love, and the greatest of these is love" (1 Cor. 13:13).

(5) For the Bible therefore, the virtue of love takes the highest consideration (Mk. 12:28-31), hence we read:

(i) "Seek after love" (1 Cor. 14:1).

(ii) "Let your love for one another be constant, for love covers a multitude of sin" (1 Pt. 4:8-11).

(iii) "Love your neighbour as yourself" (Leviticus 19:18; Mt. 22:39; James 2:8-11).

(iv) Love one another . . . Do not pay back evil with evil . . . (1 Pt. 3:8-13).

(v) "Your love must be sincere – love one another with the affection of brothers . . ." (Rom. 12:9-12).
Here in Romans 12:9-21, we read what love means in its concrete consideration.

(vi) Faith without good works is idle, if not dead (James 2:18-23).

(vii) ". . . a person is justified by his works and not by faith alone" (James 2:24).
Read Jn. 13:34; Mt. 25:31-46. To the Philippian Christians Paul said: "Live according to what you have learned and accepted, what you have heard me say and seen me do. Then will the God of peace be with you" (Phil. 4:9). St. Paul is not talking about faith here, he is exhorting the believers to practise the virtues – "all that is honest, pure, admirable, decent, virtuous or worthy of praise" (Phil. 4:8).

Faith is necessary in spiritual life but it is not sufficient for salvation. Those who believe in Jesus must act like Jesus – they must go about doing good (Acts 10:38).

# Q. 39 Does the Bible not say that we are saved by grace? Why do we talk about the sacraments?

Some people say that we are saved by grace (Rom. 3:24; Titus 2:11ff, Eph. 2:13); this is true, but God's grace comes to us in things that we can see and touch (in tangible forms) – water, bread, word, etc. as we shall read below. So besides the practice of love and concern, the Bible teaches us that we need to:

(1) take the Word of God to heart (Lk. 8:21; 11:28; Jn. 6:63).

(2) We also need to eat the Body of Christ and drink His Blood if we are to have life and be raised up on the last day (Jn. 6:51-58). Catholic Theology calls the Sacrament wherein we receive this grace 'Holy Eucharist' (Lk. 22:14-20).

(3) We need to receive "Power from on high" (That is, the Holy Spirit) if we are to truly belong to Christ and be able to bear witness to His holy Name (Lk. 24:49; Acts 2:1-41; 4:31; 10:44; Rom. 8:9). In Catholic Theology, we call the Sacrament wherein we receive this grace 'Confirmation' (For more discussion on confirmation, see Question 56).

(4) We need to be baptized in the name of Jesus (Acts 10: 48; Rom. 6:1-14; Jn. 3:1-8). We receive this grace of baptism (the new life) in what the Catholic theology calls the 'Sacrament of Baptism' (cf. Jn. 5:40).

(5) We need to be forgiven by the Church of the living God, "the pillar and bulwark of the truth" (1 Tm. 3:15) through which "the manifold Wisdom of God may be made known" (Eph. 3:10).

(6) The Power and Authority to forgive sin (a power and authority which only belongs to God) was transmitted to the Church by the Lord Himself:

> "Receive the Holy Spirit. If you forgive men's sins, they are forgiven them; if you hold them bound, they are held bound" (Jn. 20:22).

Catholic Theology calls the Sacrament wherein we receive this forgiveness 'Penance' or the 'Sacrament of Reconciliation'.

(7) In all the passages cited here, the Bible teaches us the different ways we receive the grace of God. So it is not only faith that is required for salvation. To be saved, we need the grace of the New Testament. St. John says that this saving grace of Christ comes through water, blood, and the Holy Spirit (1 Jn. 5:6-8). Concerning this blood and water, read Jn. 19:34. "In the blood and water there may also be a symbolic reference to the Eucharist and Baptism" (The New American Bible).

(8) In conclusion, we can say that to be saved from sin, the power of Satan, and eternal death (the three greatest enemies of man), what is required is faith in the Person and teaching of Christ, not just faith in His Person. Jesus tells us that if we love Him, we should keep His Commandments (Jn. 14:15-23). He does not say: "believe in me and nothing more", so, complete commitment to Christ (faith in Him) embraces:

(a) Belief in His person as the only mediator between God and man (1 Tm. 1:5; Jn. 14:5-6).

(b) Obedience to His commandments (Jn. 14:15-23).

(c) Obedience to His doctrines (Jn. 14:7; Lk. 6:46-47).

HE WHO PUTS FAITH IN JESUS AND DISREGARDS HIS TEACHING IS NOT COMMITTED TO CHRIST, BUT HE IS COMMITTED TO THAT WHICH HE LIKES IN CHRIST.

The Bible teaches us that the crown of glory will be given only to those who have kept the rules till their death (2 Tim. 2:5; Rev. 2:10; 21:7).

# Q. 40 Why does the Catholic Church love and honour the Blessed Virgin Mary? (Lk. 8:19-21; 1:28; 42-55)

(1) Those we call Saints are so because they reached a certain level of relationship with Jesus. This relationship is called union – a perfect conformity to the will of God in Christ. The Blessed Virgin Mary is such a person who was close to the Lord. The Blessed Virgin Mary in the first instance of her conception, by a singular grace and privilege of almighty God, in view of the foreseen merits of Jesus Christ the Saviour of the human race, was preserved free from all stain of original sin (Pius IX, 1854). Why was she granted this privilege? She was granted this privilege because of the role she was to play in the whole plan of salvation: she was to become the Mother of the Redeemer, the sinless one of Israel. The grace we got at baptism (freedom from Sin), the Blessed Virgin Mary got at conception. It is the same God at work in different ways.

(2) When the word of God was addressed to Mary, she took it to heart (Lk. 1:38; 11:27-28). "If we shall have the Spirit of Mary, we will possess Jesus equally as she did". Refer also to Question 18. Paul says – "Christ's message, in all its richness, must live in your hearts. Teach and instruct each other with all wisdom. Sing psalms, hymns, and sacred

songs; sing to God, with thanksgiving in your hearts. Everything you do or say, then, should be done in the name of the Lord Jesus, as you give thanks through him to God the Father" (Col. 3:16-17). This passage of Scripture perfectly describes the life of the Blessed Virgin of Nazareth. Her yes to God was total. The Magnificat (Lk. 1:46-55) reveals the virtues (moral and religious qualities) of the Blessed Mother of our God.

(3) If we can say with our whole heart and mind: "Let it be done to me according to your word" (Lk. 1:38), then we are getting close to being like the Blessed Virgin Mary. It is indeed great that she could say yes to God's wonderful promise that she would conceive a baby through the power of the Holy Spirit – a message very difficult to believe. This privilege was accompanied by trials – she bore the sufferings of her Son, right from the time of the child's birth to the time of crucifixion. In all these situations, she did not complain. What a courageous Lady!

(4) The Blessed Virgin Mary is "the most excellent fruit of the redemption", a figure of the spotless bride of Christ, which is the Church. And united to the victorious Christ in heaven, Mary is "the image and first flowering of the Church as she is to be perfected in the world to come". She SHINES forth "as a sign of sure *hope* and *solace* for the pilgrim people of God". She is a sure hope and comfort for those who feel unloved by God. Sometimes, we are forced to ask, "does God love Me? If yes, why do I go through these pains?" The Bible calls us to look at the Blessed Virgin Mary's obedient life. The life of the Blessed Virgin Mary is a sure hope and comfort for those who think that their own troubles are indications that the Lord does not really care for them. Looking at the Blessed Virgin Mary's life (humanly speaking), in what way was she blessed? Although she is addressed 'Blessed among Women', a woman that is highly favoured (Lk. 1:28; 42), without faith it is impossible to see how she is so highly favoured (Lk. 1:28; 42), without faith it is impossible to see how she is so highly favoured. Mary lives to teach us how to love God.

(5) History (Bible history, Oral tradition, Pious Writings) did not say anything against the Blessed Virgin Mary. They did not simply conceal (hide) her vice, but she was so excellent that they could not find anything evil to say about her. Peter fell, the New Testament writers recorded it for our reading. David fell, the Old Testament writers recorded it for our reading and so too were many instances of people who were chosen but who fell. The Blessed Virgin Mary was called and justified, and she remained obedient to the Lord.

(6) The Blessed Virgin Mary did not run away from the world. She was married. She got involved in the affairs of her relations. After the announcement of Christ's birth, she set out in haste to the hill country to a town of Judah to her cousin Elizabeth who was then pregnant. They both stayed for about three months before she returned to her home. (Lk. 1:39-56). Those who are privileged in this life and wish to SIT ON THRONES, commanding others to serve them and venerate them should learn from the HUMILITY of the Blessed Virgin Mary. In spite of her exalted position, she never put herself forward. One can say this:

> God has left a man (Jesus) for men to look at and learn how to live their lives. He has also left a woman (The Blessed Virgin Mary) for women to look at and learn how to live their lives. But men and women have all to learn from the life of Jesus and of the Blessed Virgin.

(7) Scripture does not say that we should follow the Blessed Virgin Mary. She is one of the redeemed (we are in fact told to imitate her, Heb. 6:12; 13:7). However, in the Scripture, we are told that the Blessed Virgin Mary is the one highly favoured and that all generations will call her Blessed. That virtue (goodness) for which Mary is praised, is what we should aim to have. When she said:

> "I am the Lord's servant, and I am willing to do whatever he wants. May everything you said come true" (Lk. 1:38). This total submission (surrender) tells us what attitude we should have in life towards God. We should have an obedient faith that puts the world beneath our feet. Our Blessed Mother whole-heartedly shared in the life, mission and sorrows of her Son. And in this close union, we see the cause of her power to intercede for those who call upon her. She knows Jesus more than anybody (Jn. 2:3-5) and she calls men to be obedient to the Son: "Do whatever He tells you" (Jn. 2:3-5).

(8) Most of what we know about Jesus' conception, birth, growth, come from the Blessed Virgin Mary. It was she who told the Evangelists what happened. The evangelists, Matthew and Luke, were not with the young girl, Mary, when the Angel of God came to her (Lk. 1:30-38).

(9) The Blessed Virgin Mary is the greatest preacher of Jesus, for it was she who brought and introduced Jesus to the world and almost the whole world is running after this her only Son. In fact, whoever believes in Jesus is a disciple of the Blessed Virgin Mary because such a person is putting faith

in what Mary says her Son is – a child with extraordinary origin. Mary told us that He was born of the Holy Spirit.

(10) Again, we were told by the Bible that Mary took care of her Son and the child was obedient to her and Joseph (Lk. 2:39-52).

(11) St. Bridget of Sweden (a woman who had 8 children) said: "Mary did not deny anything to Christ on earth. Christ will not deny anything to Mary in heaven". This is why we should ask her to pray for us.

(12) We can see why the holy Catholic Church, following the Bible, exalts the work of God in Mary and she does this by the titles she has given to her:

(a) She is the Mother of God *(Theotokos)*.

(b) She is a "Pre-eminent and singular member" of the Church, the body of Christ.

(c) She is an "excellent exemplar in faith and charity" (See The Dogmatic Constitution on the Church, Ch. 8).

(d) She is the "Immaculate Conception", "Mary, conceived without Sin" who remained till death without sin.

(e) She is Virgin before and after the birth of the only Son she had, Jesus Christ.

This is just a sketch of Mary. The Church cannot describe her enough nor love her enough.

# Q. 41 What lesson do we learn from Mary, the Mother of Jesus?

(1) The Blessed Virgin Mary knows who it is that made her what she is and knowing this, she gives thanks and praise to God. Some people live as if their life and what they have come from their personal efforts. The Psalmist already tells us that: If the Lord does not build the house, in vain does the labourer labour (Ps. 127:1-2). The Blessed Mother of our Redeemer understood this well as the Magnificat reveals (Lk. 1:46-55).

(2) The good we do in this life helps us to walk towards heaven where Mary is, but our deeds alone cannot bring us into heaven. On the whole, we are saved by the Mercy of God. The Blessed Virgin Mary more than anyone else realized this. We can see the secret of her humility. To the venerable Mary of Agreda, the Blessed Virgin Mary said:

"I lived in the greatest constraints, in poverty and detached from earthly things, most perfect and holy; and this holy Freedom I did indeed experience at the hour of my death. Consider then, my daughter, and be mindful of this living example" (The Mystical City of God, p. 775).

The Bible calls the Blessed Mother of Jesus, a "Virgin" (Lk. 1:34). And the Holy Catholic Church teaches us that the Blessed Lady remained a Virgin during and after childbirth.

(3) A Virgin before and after childbirth may seem difficult to understand just as Moses' experience of God in the desert at Sinai is difficult to understand, for the Bible says that:

"Moses saw that the bush was on fire but that it was not burning up"; and Moses said to himself: "This is strange" (Ex. 3:2-3).

What more can be said about God's love for the Blessed Mother of Our Saviour: it is "Strange". God chose her and decorated her far beyond all Creatures – angels and saints.

(4) Another wonderful event in the life of the Blessed Virgin Mary is that the Body of Jesus (His Flesh) was fashioned from the body of this immaculate Virgin of Nazareth. In view of her special relationship with her Son, our divine Saviour, the Church believes that the blessed Virgin Mary never experienced corruption – was assumed body and soul into heaven. The story of the assumption is not only a result of theological reflection; tradition upholds it (see Question 15). Venerable Mary of Agreda says:

"If in the first instant of her Conception she was the brightest Aurora, effulgent with the rays of the sun of the Divinity beyond all the brightness of the most exalted seraphim, and if afterwards she was still further illumin-ed by the contract of the hypostatic Word, who derived his humanity from her purest substance, it necessarily follows that she should be his Companion for all eternity, possessing such a likeness to Him, that none greater can be possible between a God-man and a creature." (The Mystical City of God, p. 782).

# Q. 42 Is every Christian a priest?

(1) The Bible says:

"You are priests of the King, you are holy and pure, you are God's very own – all this so that you may show to others how God called you out of the darkness into his wonderful light" (1 Pt. 2:9 – The Living Bible).

The ancient Israel were given special titles: a chosen race (Is. 44:1ff), Kingdom of priests (Ex. 19:6), a people set apart to serve the Lord (Ex. 19:6; Mal. 3:17). All these show their divine election – they were chosen servants.

(2) In the N.T., these titles are given to all those who are baptized into Christ. Why? Because the N.T. people are now the new Israel of God. As members of Christ's redeemed people, they share in Jesus rights and privileges. Baptized into Him, they can serve and worship God in Christ, thus continuing the priestly function of Christ, the eternal High Priest. But this "priesthood of the faithful" as it is called, is different from the priesthood of the ordained minister of the gospel (called Sacramental priesthood in Catholic Theology). The Bible shows that there is a difference:

(a) "Now every high priest is appointed to offer gifts and sacrifices" (Heb. 8:3).

(b) "Every high priest is taken from among men and made their representative before God, to offer gifts and sacrifices for sins ... one does not take this honour on his initiative, but only when called by God as Aaron was" (Heb. 5:1-4).

From what the Bible teaches, it shows that there are people with specific spiritual power to be exercised over the life of God's people (Matt. 16:19) both in the O.T. and in N.T.

In the O.T., there were Kings and Prophets but the Levites, descendants of Levi (Gn. 49:5; Ex. 6:16; Dt. 33:8-10), became the priestly tribe (Number 1:47-53; Judges 17:7-13). Levi was an ancestor of Jesus (Lk. 3:24).

From what has been said, we can see the two kinds of priesthood in the Bible:

(i) The Ordained Minister who is a representative of the Community of Faith (Heb. 5:1-4; 1 Tm. 3:1-13).

(ii) The priestly faithful (1 Pt. 1:9). These are called priests in view of the fact that they are incorporated into Christ, the eternal High priest. They cannot preside at the Eucharistic Celebration to "offer gifts and Sacrifices" for sin (Heb. 8:3), nor have they power to forgive sins (Jn. 20:22). They can however offer Spiritual Sacrifice by uniting in worship their own intention to that of the ordained priest.

# Q. 43 Whose duty is it to discipline in a faith community and interpret the Bible?

(1) The Lord said that the time was coming when He would make a new Covenant with His people; He would put His law within them and write it on their hearts.

"None of them will have to teach his fellow countryman to know the Lord, because all will know me, from the least to greatest" (Jer. 31:31-34).

From what the Bible says here, it would seem that nobody should, in fact, take it upon himself to teach another the Word of God since each person will know God personally.

But the Bible also says:

"Let not many of you become teachers" (James 3:1). This presupposes that some people will be teachers of God's Word.

(2) In the Jewish Communities of Jesus' time, the scribes and the Pharisees were the teachers of faith and morals. Jesus told the crowds during His preaching ministry:

"do everything and observe everything they tell you. But do not follow their example. Their words are bold but their deeds are few" (Mt. 22:3-4).

(3) It is clear then from the Bible that there are people whose duty it is to teach the Word of God (1 Tim 5:17). The Lord said to his apostle Peter:

"I will entrust to you the keys of the Kingdom of heaven. Whatever you declare bound on earth shall be bound in heaven; whatever you declare loosed on earth shall be loosed in heaven" (Mt. 16:18-19).

NAB commenting on this says:

"Simon Peter is the keeper of the keys, the one who has power to open and to close, to "bind" and to "loose", to allow and to forbid" (cf. Is. 22:22).

The exercise of this responsibility is here compared to the disciplinary and doctrinal authority of the Rabbis who in Jesus time interpreted the Old Testament for the faith and the life of the people (NAB on Mt. 16:19).

(4) In the early Church, there were different classes of Ministers (Eph. 4:11):

  (i) Presbyters (elders) (1 Tim. 5: 17-25).
  (ii) Episcopos (Bishop) (1 Tim. 3:1-7).
  (iii) Deacons (1 Tim. 3:8-13).

The function of the Presbyter is not exactly that of a Bishop. The early presbyters possessed the responsibility of preaching and teaching while the Bishop was responsible for administration (pastoral care of the people), to restrain false and useless teaching and to ordain Ministers of the gospel (Titus 1:9-10; 1 Tm. 5:22; 6:20).

(5) In the Bible, we read that the Lord gives the Church apostles, prophets, evangelists, pastors and teachers. These "build up the body of Christ, till we become one in faith and in the knowledge of God's Son, and form that perfect man who is

Christ come to full stature" (Eph. 4:11-13). They do so through their good life teaching and discipline.

(6) The work of interpreting authentic doctrine, particularly when there is doubt or error so as to restrain false and useless teaching, is *properly speaking*, that of the Episcopos (the Bishop) as we read in Titus 1:9 and their immediate co-operators, the ordained ministers of the gospel. The Bishop is called "God's Steward" (Titus 1:7).

(7) In Titus 1:6ff and Acts 20:17, 28, the terms episcopos and presbyteros ("bishop" and "presbyter") refer to the same persons (NAB on Titus 1:5-9). Both Timothy and Titus were first century Bishops.

# Q. 44  Am I not free to read the Bible?

(1) You are free to read the Bible to draw INSPIRATION from it. The Bible teaches us that:

"All Scripture is inspired by God and is useful for teaching the truth, rebuking error, correcting faults and giving instructions for right living, so that the person who serves God may be fully qualified and equipped to do every kind of good deed" (2 Tm. 3:16-17).

And again:

(2) "Everything written in the Scriptures was written to teach us, in order that we might have hope through the patience and encouragement which the Scriptures give us" (Rom. 15:3-4).

Considering what the Bible says here, we should reflect on what it teaches for our daily encouragement and consolation and for a robust Christian faith and life.

(3) But the Bible is not all that easy to read and interpret. Some people think that each person is free to interpret the Bible in his own way but this kind of view sometimes is held by those who search the Bible for certain particular interests; they are not interested to know the truth which the Bible wishes to teach; their concern is whether the Bible can support their view.

(4) The Bible is a book containing prophecies of all sorts (2 Pt. 1:20-21) and as we read it, we shall discover a great deal of statements in the books which would appear to contradict one another. We therefore need a guide to resolve the seeming contradictions we may come across. Think of this:

(i) Leviticus gives instructions as to which animals we should not eat (Lev. 11:1-47).

(ii) 1 Corinthians 10:25-27 tells us: "You are free to eat anything sold in the meat market". And again "Eat what is set before you"

     (iii) The Lord said to the seventy-two: "Eat what is set before you" (Lk. 10:7).

     (iv) According to St. Mark's gospel, Jesus declared all foods clean. (Mk. 7:19).

(5) Now, looking at the conflict between the teachings of Leviticus and Paul and Jesus, it is obvious that a problem has arisen, namely the interpretation of the relevant texts of the Scripture passages in question. And no one can assume the work of this interpretation unless he has the training to do it. The Church of the Living God has the training and power to do this. It is her proper work (1 Tm. 3:15; 4:13; Eph. 3:10).

# Q. 45 Can anyone judge an ordained minister of the gospel of Christ?

**First, What does it mean to judge someone?**

(1) In the Bible, to "judge" means to condemn somebody; to declare him or her to be evil. This is not the same thing as to rebuke somebody's wrongful action. To perform some evil actions does not make one an evil person. Therefore, it is wrong to condemn a child of God – to say that such a person is evil; to hold such a view is to put the person in the same condition as Satan, the prince of evil. Jesus teaches us not to condemn:

"Do not judge" (Mt. 7:1) and Paul asks: "Who are you to pass judgment on another's servant? His master alone can judge whether he stands or falls. And stand he will, for the Lord is able to make him stand" (Rom. 14:4).

The Divine Master Himself says: "God did not send the Son into the world to condemn the world . . ." (Jn. 3:17). If God who has the absolute right to do this does not do it, how then can man judge his fellow man?

(2) We should refrain from venturing to pass judgment, for we are likely to make mistakes when we do this, for "man looks on the outward appearance, but the Lord looks on the heart" (1 Sam. 16:7).

(3) *We should not judge priests of Christ.* St. Ambrose says:

"Do not consider their outward appearance, but the grace of their ministries. It was in the presence of angels that you spoke, as it is written: "The lips of a priest guard knowledge, and men seek instruction from his mouth, for he is the angel of the Lord of hosts. There is no place for deception nor for denial: he is the angel who proclaims the Kingdom of Christ and eternal life. You must not make your assessment of him according to his appearance, but according to his office. Consider what he transmitted, reflect upon his function, recognize his dignity" (St. Ambrose, Treatise on the Mysteries, Quoted in the Roman Breviary III, pp. 298-299).

## Q. 46 Can anyone in the Lord sin?
### No one is good but God alone" (Mk. 10:18)

St. John says:

(1) "We know that no child of God keeps on sinning, for the Son of God keeps him safe, and the Evil One cannot harm him" (1 Jn. 5:18).

(2) A child of God does not remain in sin (1 Jn. 3:9).

It is clear from what the Bible says here that anyone who is in the Lord cannot remain in sin. Take note of the words "remain in sin". Such a person has power to overcome sinful inclinations (Phil. 4:13; 1 Cor. 15:10).

It is important to know that even though one feels that one does not sin, still no one can be absolutely certain that he is not in sin. St. Paul knew that it would be unwise for him to justify himself (1 Cor. 4:1-4). He left the judgment as to whether or not he is standing to the Lord, for only the Lord, according to the Bible, knows who are his (2 Tim. 2:19-20).

Commenting on Rom. 6:12-19, NAB says, "while the Christian remains in this mortal life, the power of sin in him is not fully overcome; his personal effort under the influence of grace is required to surmount the weakness remaining in him".

(3) A Christian is not God. A Christian is not steel. The Bible warns us to guide against over-confidence. "Let anyone who thinks he is standing upright watch out lest he fall!" (1 Cor. 10:12). There is nobody who is above sinning as long as he or she still lives in the flesh. Prov. 24:16 says though the good man may fall seven times, he is soon up; which presupposes that a good man may sometimes fall. The Bible bears witness to the fact that even after Pentecost, Peter and Barnabas and some of the Jewish Christians were found guilty of *insincerity*, an offence which would send one to the confessional today (Galatian 2:11-14).

(4) The Bible exhorts us: "Never let evil talk pass your lips; say only the good things men need to hear, things that will really help them" (Eph. 4:29-31); and again ... bless and do not curse (Rom. 12:14-21) yet we read that St. Paul "burst out of anger – and said to the high priest Ananias:

"You are the one God will strike, you whitewashed wall (Acts 23:2-3).

Does the action of St. Paul here show that He has taken up the Spirit of Christ? We are not encouraging sinning; we only wish to show that we can never be wholly innocent. Jesus told a man: "No one is good but God alone" (Mk. 10:18). In spite of being a man of the Spirit, St. Paul was still sensitive to discourtesy (See Acts 15:36-40).

(5) What kind of sin a child of God is not likely to commit?

The Bible says that there is a sin which is deadly (1 Jn. 5:16-17). It is not clear what this sort of sin is. Modern theologians make the following distinctions about sin and from this distinction, we might know which kind of sin a child of God would not commit:

(i.a) There are sins which reverse our fundamental option for God. Perhaps this is apostasy (NAB on 1 Jn. 5:16-17). Such sin may come from hardness of heart (Heb. 3:8) – a conscious, practical, disregard of divine message (Ps. 95:7-11). There is no child of God who will live in this way. (See Richard P. McBrian, *Catholicism: Study Edition*, pp. 1336ff).

(i.b) There are also people who see the works of God and knowingly credit such works to satan. In its nature, this is a very serious sin, for such people are sinning against the Holy Spirit (Mk. 3:29). It is called mortal sin in Catechism. The Pharisees were jealous of Jesus and attributed His healing work to the work of the devil (Read Mk. 3:22-30). It is clear that those who are in the Lord will not commit this sort of sin.

(ii) There are sins which reflect poorly on our commitment to God but which do not reverse our course towards God. Such sins are serious but one can do away with them since the sinner in that condition more often than not desires to become a good child of God. The case of the woman with bad name in Luke's gospel may be an example. Jesus forgave her many sins (Lk. 7:36ff; Numbers 12:1-14).

(iii) There are less serious sins. Catholic Theology calls them venial sins (1 Jn. 5:17).

(iv) Below all these are what can be described as imperfections ("I didn't laugh" – Sarah's denial) (Gn. 18:15).

Having seen the different categories of sin, the question is:

(a) Can a child of God be guilty of Sin in Category (i.a. + b); that is, is it possible for one who is abiding in the Lord, a child of God as the Bible calls such a person, to turn back and say: "There is no God, everything the Bible says is not true", a practical denial of God and His Saving message? We do not think this is possible.

(b) Could one who is abiding in the Lord turn to the practice of sin; choose a whole life of sin? We do not see how this is possible.

(c) What about sin in category (ii-iii)? It is possible however, for one who is abiding in the Lord (a child of God) to act, at one time or the other, insincerely as we read that the apostle Peter did (Gal. 2:11-14).

(6) Another hard position: Some people say that one should be sure of Salvation.

Some people believe and teach others that a child of God should be sure that he is saved; that he or she has no more sin. This sort of teaching has a history. Dr. Martin Luther (17.7.1505), Professor of theology in the University of Wittenberg, believed and taught that the justification that brings salvation is faith in the God of promise, to Christ the mediator. Accusing Catholics of stressing DEED and also being unsure of salvation, he offered for his followers certainty of salvation and joy of the Spirit; He said that one should "cling to God who cannot lie . . ." (Pfurther Stephanus, O.P. *Luther and Aquinas, a conversation*, p. 22). For Luther, to doubt one's salvation is to doubt:

"God's power and mercy" (Ibid., p. 22), or "not to believe in divine promise" (Ibid., p. 26). So, if we doubt God's grace and do not believe that God is well pleased with us for Christ's sake, then we deny that Christ has redeemed us, indeed we question absolutely all his mercies' (Ibid., p. 23).

This is Luther's theory of salvation, the hinges of his spirituality. One should be certain that one is saved because through faith, we are sons of God in Christ Jesus (Gal. 3:26). Catholicism, Luther further says, makes a religion of redemption (turned it into) one of achievement on man's good conduct. This thought of Martin Luther shocked ecclesiastical ears so much that the Council of Trent took time to answer Luther. It quickly recognised the whole question as an inseparable part of the article of Justification.

(7) **The Catholic Reaction – The Council of Trent**

On the decree of Justification (Session VI, Cap. 9) it says: "No one can know with certainty of faith, in which there can be no error, that he has obtained God's grace" (Ibid., p. 27).

(8) Catholic theology teaches us that if a man does not place an obstacle on his way, the sacraments confer (saving) sanctifying grace. In that case, one would be sure of salvation because the sacraments work irrespective of the moral

condition of the priest who celebrates it. (Duns Scotus followers used this argument).

(9) But this pertains to the Sacrament. The question is: How do we know that a man does not place obstacle on his way? The Council further asks: What does Christ say about the talents? Does Paul not say that we should work out our salvation in fear and trembling (Phil. 2:12); and that we should be alert or else the one who thinks that he is standing may be approaching his fall (1 Cor. 10:12)? The conclusion of the Council is this: IF A PERSON HAS TO CO-OPERATE IN THE REALIZATION OF HIS SALVATION, THERE CANNOT BE PERSONAL CERTAINTY.

(10) St. Thomas Aquinas said: A Christian can be certain of his hope only when he possesses charity and remains morally good.

(11) It could be true, and to be relied on, that no one can go on sinning if he has an unwavering faith in God's mercy and power. But the prudent and just man however, should remain in a 'chaste fear' (Timor castus) of losing God; because what we must fear to lose, we cannot be certain of possessing or attaining (Summa theology, 11-11, 18,4).

(12) Catholic theologians (teachers of faith) tell us that God's encounter with man in the person of Jesus Christ brings an inward transformation, a change; nevertheless, this "regeneration by which God justifies us is no magical transformation. It truly occurs within us in our movements and reactions by ridding us of our attachments to ourselves and our glory and by binding us to Jesus Christ in faith" (Xavier Leon Dufour). One can stop sinning by word, deed or omission and be *absolutely* sure of Salvation only if one is completely obedient to God's will (Jn. 15:1-5).

The truth however is, who can say:
"I am without sin"? (Jn. 8:7).

(13) It is advisable for us to hope to be saved (Rm. 8:23-25; Col. 1:27; Heb. 6:19). But we cannot declare ourselves acquitted (justified) before our final judgment. It is God who will judge us whether we have lived well or not. We must learn from St. Paul. To the Corinthian Christians, he said:

"I will not pass judgment on myself. True, my conscience does not report me at all, but THAT DOES NOT PROVE THAT I AM ACQUITTED: the Lord alone is my judge. There must be no passing of premature judgment, leave that until the Lord comes" (1 Cor. 4:4-5)

Let those who say to themselves: "I am saved", "I am all right", take note of the above Bible passage.

# Q. 47 What does it mean to be humble?

(1) HUMILITY: Lk. 14:7-11; Mt. 18:1-4; Phil. 2:1-11. Humility means freedom from pride and arrogance.

(2) Let us start with a story from an incident in the Bible.

Paul and Barnabas did not want to be DEIFIED (Acts 14:5-18). Their actions were such that the people of Lystra and Derbe thought that they were 'gods' in human forms. Paul had tried to convince the people that divine power works through his word and to convince the people, he cures the cripple. However, the pagan tradition of the occasional appearance of gods among men leads the people astray in interpreting the miracle. The incident reveals the cultural difficulties with which the Church had to cope (NAB on Acts 14:5-18). When the people tried to see the whole event with their pagan dusty eyes, Paul, through his action (for the Scripture says that he tore his garment, rushed into the crowd shouting – all as a protest), teaches us his basic insight and conviction, namely, that Power, Strength, and every good thing comes from the Lord, and that he himself could do all things only in the power of the Lord who strengthened him (Phil. 4:13; Phil. 1:29; Eph. 2:1-10). In his apostolate, Paul says: "I work and struggle, impelled by that energy of his which is so powerful a force within me" (Col. 1:29). This realization that the power that works mightily in him comes from the Lord, is an act of humility.

(3) The realization that every good thing we have comes through the Lord's help, is humility. A humble person talks in the manner of the author of the letter to the Hebrews: "God permitting, we shall advance" (Heb. 6:3).

(4) A humble person does not have a high opinion of himself. He does not size up himself with others. He knows that gifts are different. He knows that he is not better than someone else because of what he has. The humble man recognizes that they are better, who live the right sort of life.

(5) St. Paul exhorts us to be humble:

"All of you must put on the apron of humility, to serve one another; God resists the proud, but shows favour to the humble. Humble yourselves, then, under God's mighty hand, so that he will lift you up in his own good time" (1 Pet. 5:5-7).

(6) Humility is a mark of true conversion and of holiness.

The mark of true conversion is whether or not one is humble. When the Jewish authorities sent some priests and Levites to John to ask him: "Who are you?" John, a popular preacher, would have told the people "Yes, I am the Messiah". No, he did not mix up his word. He made his point clear:

"I am not the Messiah"

"I am not Elijah"

"Are you the Prophet"?

"I am not what you think that I am. I don't measure up to what you are thinking". "I am only the Voice of the one you are thinking about" (Jn. 1:19-23). John the Baptist was a humble man. Whose voice was he? He made it clear that he was the voice of "a man who is coming after me, but he is greater than I am, because he existed before I was born" (Jn. 1:30). In St. Luke's gospel, he says: "I am not good enough even to untie his sandals" (Lk. 3:16). "He must become more important while I become less important" (Jn. 3:30).

(7) We find from experience that people are not sincere enough to say to themselves: "I am not . . ." or "I cannot do such and such: you do it because you have the gift". Although we must be careful here because there are people who, though gifted, would want to avoid responsibility and then refuse to do something, to take upon themselves jobs that demand their time and energy. What we are guarding against in discussing humility is a prideful desire to be heard, to be seen, to be regarded as important, to edge out (chase away) a more competent person from doing what he or she has got the talent to do or of parading ourselves as more important than other people. Humility enjoins us to avoid such a godless conduct, for that sort of desire is evil; it is robbery to assume what we are not or to wish to be taken to be a person of a certain kind that we are not.

(8) A humble man is one who knows that he is what he is by the grace of God, and that of his own power alone, he cannot do any good thing. In other words, it is the humble person who realizes his utter dependence on God.

The Bible says:

"No one can have anything unless God gives it to him" (Jn. 3:27).

Paul realized this truth in his own life and he acknowledged it. He knew how bad he was (He was breathing murderous threats against the Lord's disciples, Acts 9:1). He knew that his position, all he had and treasured was a gift. "I do not even deserve to be called an apostle, because I persecuted God's Church. But by God's grace I am what I am, and the grace that he gave me was not without effect. On the contrary, I have worked harder than any of the other apostles, although it was not really my own doing, but God's grace working with me" (1 Cor. 15:9-11). In this statement, he helps us to understand what humility means.

85

In St. Paul, we see a man who knew that of himself, he could do nothing and that what he is and did, is the effect of God's loving gift. The Psalmist came to the same realization that if the Lord does not build the house, the work of the builders is useless; if the Lord does not protect the city, in vain does the watch man keep vigil (Ps. 127:1). Writing about her own life, St. Theresa of the Little Flower said: "I did not deserve the graces heaven showered on me. I had many faults. It's true that I longed to be good, but I had an odd way of going about it" (The autobiography Ch. 5). James says every gift is from the Lord of heaven (James 1:9-11; 17; 4:6).

(9) Humble children of God never boast about themselves or their achievements. They know that no one deserves this or that favour. They know that our being and fruitfulness is the Lord's own doing (Hosea 14:8). This knowledge is humility. The logical opposite of a humble man is the Vain Man. Who are vain men?

"Vain men, are silly, not realizing their own LIMITA-TIONS. This comes out in glaring fashion when they take on an important job for which they are not qualified, and are proved incompetent. It is a type which affects showy clothes and a smart manner and that sort of thing. They tell the world what successful men they are and make that the topic of their conversation, as if that would win respect for them ..." (Aristotle, NE Bk. 4, Ch. 3, p. 126).

(10) No doubt, if a person is gifted, successful and good (virtuous), he deserves to be honoured. But he is not to look for this honour. If a person were to bully on us because we have not honoured him, then he lacks the virtue of humility. Without the virtue of humility, it is hard to beat good fortune modestly. "Accordingly such persons, unable to support the favours of fortune (blessings of this life) without pressumption and fancying themselves above the rest of mankind, look down on everyone else, although their own behaviour is no better than that of ordinary mortals" (NE Bk. 4, Ch. 3, p. 123). Vain men are easily carried away by their gifts – material or spiritual. The humble, certainly not.

(11) To one of the brethren, appeared a devil, transformed into an angel of light, who said to him: "I am the Angel Gabriel, and I have been sent to you". But the brother said to him: "Think again, you must have been sent to somebody else. I have not done anything to deserve an angel. Immediately the devil ceased to appear" (Thomas Merton, *Desert Fathers*, p. 54). The proud man will be tempted to welcome such a vision and from then on look down on others for not having

a vision of angels; he may even go so far as to regard himself to be good, hence he had a vision.

(12) The proud are always quarrelling. Why? Because a person who thinks much about himself and little of another is impatient of the latter's fault" (Prov. 13:10).

(13) David's life teaches us the blessing of humility (Ps. 50:5-6; 2 Sm. 16:5-14). God absolved him because he was humble. Humility leads to exaltation (Glory); pride leads to hell.

(14) Do away with Spiritual Pride (Lk. 17:9-14).

In the presence of God, upright Job was unhappy with himself and he repented in dust and ashes (Job. 1:20; 42:5, 6). In the presence of God, Isaiah, Israel's sublime prophet found out how unclean he and his people were (Is. 6:1-5, 64:6). In the presence of the Lord, Peter, the apostle learned his sinfulness (Lk. 5:8). In the presence of the risen Saviour, Paul, the great apostle to the Gentiles, called himself "the Chief of Sinners" (1 Tm. 1:15). Some people say that they have no sin and so scorn the use of the sacrament of reconciliation. This of course, is lack of the virtue of humility. Such people are the ones who should go first for confession, for they are really the sinners, having thus committed the sin of calling God a liar. "The really unforgivable sin is the denial of sin, because by its nature, there is now nothing to forgive" (Fulton Sheen).

(15) Some of the Jews in Jesus time had thought they were all right and they came to Jesus to report the disaster that had taken place among the Galileans whom Pilate murdered in the Middle of their Sacrifices. Jesus answered them, "Because these Galileans were killed in that way, do you think it proves that they were worse sinners than all the other Galileans? No! I tell you that if you do not turn from your sins, you will all die as they did".

(16) The humble man will survive the evil days since he has anchored his life on the Lord, depending on Him, acknowledging Him as the source of his life, blessings and glory. One day, the devil appeared to a monk and tried to strangle the monk but he couldn't. And he said to the monk: "I suffer great violence from you, Macarius, because I cannot overcome you. For see, I do all the things that you do.

(a) You fast      (a) I eat nothing at all

(b) You watch    (b) I never sleep

"There is one thing in which you overcome me." Abbot Macarius said to him: "What is that?" The devil replied: "Your humility, for: because of it I cannot overcome you" (Desert Fathers, p. 53).

(17) "I am what I am because I am good" – this is not true.

When you acknowledge the Sovereignty of God over you and think of nothing you own as due to your goodness, you are humble, or when you consider your neighbour as better (on condition that he is better) than yourself (Phil. 2:3), then you are humble. The humble person does not feel that he deserves to be blessed more than others.

(18) Christian Spirituality calls us to die to self; that we should live no longer for ourselves but for Him who died to save us.

(19) Jesus was humble. He did not cling to His equality with God. He humbled Himself and became as it were, a SLAVE. We are fond of letting others know that we are superior. God did not do this. What an example! Jesus renounced self-affirmation and power. He did not Lord it over people. He listened to everyone who cared to talk with him. He did not impose His ideas on others. You were free to take it. I point out two incidents in the Bible that show the humility and gentleness of Christ. First when he taught the doctrine of the Bread of Life, Jesus already made it clear:

(a) "Look, I don't accept *human praise*" (Jn. 5:41). This desire for human praise is the root of our haughtiness and pride. We crucify others when they disagree with us.

(b) "Do you want to leave me too" (Jn. 6:66-69). Someone asked one of the ancient Fathers how he might obtain true humility and he answered: By keeping your eyes off other people's faults and fixing them on your own". (Alphonse Rodriguez).

(c) Seek no human praise. That frees you from pride.

(d) Keep your eyes away from people's faults.

The Humble person knows Himself – What he is; what he can do, what he cannot do. He is aware of who is his better and acknowledges this fact. This realization brings one salvation. Take note that:

(e) Pride changes angels into devils; humility makes men into angels (Augustine of Hippo).

(f) Too much humility is pride. If you reject the qualities you possess, you are not true to yourself.

Prophet Micah says what God requires of us is to do justice, Love kindness and walk humbly with your God (Micah 6:8).

(20) How to determine whether or not You are humble:

(a) If you forgive a person who has injured you before the person asks for pardon, you are humble.

(b) If you are not ashamed to ask for forgiveness when you offend someone, then you are humble.

(c) If you don't know something and you don't feel it a disgrace to ask someone who knows better than you, then of course, you are humble.

(d) If you sincerely judge that somebody else is better than you are in certain areas of life (in beauty or performance etc), then you are humble.

(e) If you bear insult and feel within yourself that you deserve to suffer because you are a sinner or because by it you are sharing in the sufferings of Christ, then of course, you are humble.

(f) If you are willing to learn what you don't know from someone lower in rank than you, you are humble.

(g) If you accept truth from your enemy, you are certainly humble.

When can someone be said to be proud?

When you feel within you and believe that you are what you are because you are good or you merit to be what you are, then you are proud.

(21) An elder fasted for 70 weeks, eating once a week. He was asking God to reveal to him a certain Bible passage but he had no revelation. So he said to himself: "Look at all the work I have done without getting anywhere! I will go to one of the brothers and ask him. On his way, an angel of the Lord was sent to him saying: "The 70 weeks you fasted did not bring you any closer to God, but now that you have humbled yourself and set out to ask your brother, I am sent to reveal the meaning of that text. And opening to him the meaning which he sought, he went away" (Ibid. p. 54).

(22) The Bible teaches us that the Lord saves "those who are humble, but humbles those who are proud" (Ps. 18:27).

# Q. 48 What is pride?

(1) The greatest evil that a man can do to his life, is to allow himself to be caught up by pride. Pride is such a deadly disease so much so that even the word of God, the word of hope, says that "THERE IS NO CURE FOR THE PROUD MAN'S MALADY, SINCE AN EVIL GROWTH HAS TAKEN ROOT IN HIM" (Ecc. 3:28-30). Pride, as one of the saints also tells us, dies fifteen minutes after we are declared dead (that is, Pride still lingers on the dead for a whole fifteen minutes after the proud man's death). What a deadly

disease of the soul! May the Lord Jesus, the humble servant of God, who remained obedient to his Father even though he was equal to Him, save us from pride.

(2) Pride is a feeling of self-importance; a display of one's superiority. We have a good example of it in the gospel. Jesus said that two men went up to the temple to pray; one was a Pharisee, the other a tax collector. The Pharisee with his head unbowed (with his head filled with pride) prayed in this fashion: "I give you thanks, O God, that I am not like the rest of men – grasping, crooked, adulterous or even like this tax collector here". The Tax Collector, not even daring to raise his eyes to heaven, kept his distance, beat his breast and said "O God, be merciful to me, a sinner" (Lk. 18:9-14). Everyone who raises himself will be brought down; but he who sincerely brings himself low, will be raised, so says the Master (Lk. 14:7-11).

(3) There is a genuine pride and this is when a person acknowledges what God has done and is still doing and will still do for him. By acknowledging God as the giver of all good things, a man shows himself forth as a 'debtor'. Certainly, "EVERY WORTHWHILE GIFT, EVERY GEN-UINE BENEFIT, COMES FROM ABOVE, DESCENDING FROM THE FATHER OF THE HEAVENLY LUMINAR-IES" (Father of all lights, physical and spiritual) James 1:16. Let us bear this in mind and not be carried away by our own self-importance.

(4) The question one must ask oneself: Am I a proud man? If we are really sincere to ourselves, we will, through the Light of the Holy Spirit, come to the realization that in some way, we are proud. If a man should ever strike his chest and boast because of what he is, or because of what he has (whether he entertains this thought of his own importance in his heart, or says it out), clearly enough, such a man is a proud person.

Our pride stems from the fact that we want men to know that we are such and such a person. Spiritual theology teaches us that pride does us harm. If we are good or if we have anything enviable, men will certainly know this, but if they do not know, we should not worry about this. It pays us nothing to be glorified by men. St. Thomas Aquinas, my brother in St. Dominic, said that it does not matter if men do not know us, but what matters is that we know ourselves. It is advisable for us to throw out pride from our life. Scripture says: "God resists the proud but bestows his favour on the lowly" (James 4:6).

(5) One lesson we might learn when we read the history of the saints is that the nearer a man comes to God, the more aware he is of the reality of his own indigence (his extreme poverty), his dependence and powerlessness. We are mere 'hangers', Custodians of God's gifts. We are something because of God's loving kindness to us. God is, "He who is; whilst we are those who are not; and we are in need of everything" (Dialogue of St. Catherine of Siena). We should realise this and never allow ourselves to be swept away by pride, the great disease that killed Lucifer, the patron of intellectual pride. Again, remember that it was because of Tyre's pride that "its destiny was cut off from God's people and its doom was sealed" (Ezekiel 28:1-19).

(6) A man of pride must eventually collapse just as the tower of Babel collapsed because of pride (Gn. 11:1-9).

### Overcoming pride calls for death to self

(7) The practice of any virtue calls for all other virtues, especially the virtue of courage and prudence (the virtue of practical wisdom, calculation or discernment). Patience is required to end well a serious job one has begun. On the whole, the exercise of any virtue is often accompanied by pain – It is death to the self that always seeks honour and praise. This death is the way to newness, to fullness of life. "Unless a grain of wheat falls to the earth and dies, it remains just a grain of wheat. But if it dies, it produces much fruit" (Jn. 12:24). A certain man was about to depart this life. His friends were sad but his last words to them were:

"I have been dying for twenty years. Now I am going to live". (James Burns)

Self annihilation leads to glory. Yes if we die with the Lord, we shall live with Him (2 Tm. 2:11-13).

Saint Jerome said:

"He does not perish who dies to live again".

*A proud man cannot resist an insult* – The beautitudes teach us to bear insults and not to retaliate. When the Lord commands this, it cannot be practised by those who are still the SLAVES of anger and pride. If pride is locked up in a person, he cannot be indifferent to injury and insults; but those who have put their flesh to death, are the ones that can practise the precepts of the New Testatment.

# Q. 49 What should be the Christian attitude in the world of fashion?

(1) At the time of John the Baptist, people were wearing expensive dresses but John chose a different value and Jesus

remarked on it (Matt. 11:2-9). To chase unquestionably the values of this life (money, possessions, dress, intellectual power) is simply an idolatry – the worship of false gods. The Bible does not hesitate to condemn such an attitude. It is "the life of empty show" (1 Jn. 2:15-17).

(2) The important question is: Is it wrong to dress up properly? Of course, the answer is No, it is not wrong nor is it a sin to dress up properly. We are not told that Jesus or the Blessed Virgin, His beloved Mother, went about improperly dressed. Right reason commands us to be properly dressed, to appear decent among humans.

(3) However, we have to bear in mind what the Bible says to married women about dressing and I think this applies to everyone. The Bible says: "The affectation of an elaborate hairdress, the wearing of golden jewelry, or the donning of rich robes is not for you. Your adornment is rather hidden character of the heart, expressed in the unfading beauty of a calm and gentle disposition" (1 Pt. 3:3-6; 1 Tim. 2:9-10; 1 Sm. 16:7-8).

(4) What the Bible wants women to do here is to avoid the love of pompous dress. The advice is: do not dress elaborately. Perhaps we do not know what counts as elaborate or too much in such a matter. Everyone has to decide this according to what the Spirit of the living God says to her in the person's heart. In any case, it is necessary to think before we act because our actions have so much to say to people.

(5) We can safely say this about dressing in general: It is not wrong to dress properly. God is not going to love us more because of the dress we wear. He is our Father who loves us already and who wishes all men to be saved. What pleases Him is that we do away with sinful, earthly things that people boast about – sexual sins, impurity, lust and shameful desires (Col. 3:5).

### Right Attitude in Judging

(6) In judging what people wear and how they behave, we should bear in mind the words of Scripture: "God does not see as man sees; man looks at appearances but the Lord looks at the heart" (1 Sam. 16:7). And again: the Word of God tells us that we should stop evaluating Christians by what the world thinks about them or by what they seem to be like on the outside (2 Cor. 5:16). Appearance is deceptive. One could be well-dressed and still be prayerful, kind, patient, chaste, in love with God and neighbour and even may be far better in the sight of God than the Christian, who in pursuit of holiness, does not wear fine clothes. Take note of this:

"When someone becomes a Christian, he becomes a brand new person INSIDE. A new life has begun" (2 Cor. 5:17, The Living Bible). The Bible is very much concerned with interior renewal.

(7) It is important however, that we Christians should not be lost in the world of fashion and superficiality. In everything we do, we should try to live in such a way that no one will ever be offended or kept back from finding the Lord by the way we act (2 Cor. 6:3).

## Q. 50  What is the right attitude to prayer of petition? (Lk. 10:38-42; 11:5-13)

### 1. Never stop praying

(Your unceasing desire is your unceasing prayer)

Scripture over and over again tells us to pray and not to lose faith in the Lord, the giver of all good things. "Have no anxiety about anything". Paul says, "but in everything by prayer and supplication with thanksgiving, let your requests be made known to God. And the peace of God which passes all understanding, will keep your hearts and your minds in Christ Jesus" (Phil. 4:6-7). Prayer brings us into contact with God. Prayer brings us His manifold blessings, the extent of which we do not know. The son of God, Christ the Lord, the Good Shepherd, urges us to ask (Mt. 7:7) for what we need. In His Loving providence, our God will never deny us anything which He, in His infinite wisdom and knowledge, knows that will be good for us for our present life and our glorification – our entry into the Joys of His Kingdom. Jesus Himself prayed for His needs. Luke said that He prayed the whole night before doing anything. For example, before He surrendered Himself to the Jews, He prayed (Lk. 22:40-46). Every action of Jesus is an example for us who are His followers. He prayed. We too should pray because in prayer, we get in touch with our Loving Father; and no one remains his old self after a meaningful prayer. "He lives well who prays well". To pray is to stand in the presence of God expressing to Him the deep desires of our heart. And if we do not go to God in prayer, to whom shall we go? We can never take control of our lives. And so we should turn to God in prayer. To pray is to submit ourselves and our plans to God. "Watch and pray", our Lord says, "that you may not enter into temptation, for the spirit indeed is willing but the flesh is weak" (Mt. 26:41). St. Augustine says: "Whoever prays, resists but whoever does not pray succumbs". Never stop praying.

In His teaching on prayer, our Lord urges us to knock; not only to knock, but to keep on knocking. In prayer, we talk to God and if we are really His children, we should never stop talking to Him. Nothing about us, somebody has rightly pointed out, is too small or too great for His Fatherly concern. "But we must bring to prayer a greater confidence that we shall be heard, for there are many graces which God inspires us (moves our minds) to ask and which we do not obtain by reason of our lack of trust" (St. Catherine de Ricci).

God certainly knows what we need but He too loves to enter into a loving dialogue with us. And so the point here is not that we are dealing with an unwilling and hard God who wants us to beg, to coerce and squeeze things from his Hands. We know that this is not so. God loves us and gives us gifts even when we do not pray. There are some things which we have received not because we spent days and months praying for them. God simply gives us some of these things purely out of His loving graciousness. But we have to ask God for our needs because we are rational beings; we are not vegetables to be fed and watered whether we like it or not. Besides, we have to pray, for according to Spiritual theologians, there are SOME THINGS WHICH GOD IN HIS DIVINE PROVIDENCE AND DISPOSITION HAS DETERMINED TO GIVE US ONLY IF WE PRAY. We do not know what those things are; so, we've got to keep on knocking. Your prayers may seem fruitless now; but be sure of this: that every prayer offered with, and through Jesus Christ, will be amply rewarded in a WAY and at a TIME we do not know. No prayer is useless. So, my dear friends, never stop praying.

What is needed is that we pray ceaselessly and with TRUST. We must seek the Lord's will and live in union with Him – surrender and accept results according to His divine providence, knowing that He loves us. If He has given us His Son, what else can He not give us? Anything which He knows that will contribute to our final glorification – salvation in Christ – He will give; He will not give us what will lead us to everlasting suffering, no matter how much we treasure such things and cry for them. His love for us is so great that He will never deny us anything which He knows will lead us into everlasting happiness. Never stop praying.

(2) **Use "Few Words"**

The Lord said to His disciples:

"In your prayers do not babble as the pagans do, for they think that by using *many* words they will make themselves heard. Do not be like them" (Mt. 6:7-8).

Do not rattle like the unbelievers. Do not show off like the showmen, the Pharisees. What is wrong with their prayer? *"They think that they will win a hearing by the sheer multiplication of words"* (Mt. 6:7). Lk. 20:47 – says "they make a show of saying long prayers".

God is not deaf. He is not won over by hundreds of words. It is the heart turned towards God that is far more important than a thousand words from the mouth of the faithless, sinful man. Read the story of Anna in the Old Testament. She spoke in her heart (1 Sam. 1:9-16).

It is a grievous mistake to think that because we have said more, God will hear us. This is like saying of God: "He wasn't sure, so I have convinced Him now". Let us listen to THREE authorities on prayer:

St. Cyprian – "We should not inflate our prayers with a flurry of words, nor laugh in a torrent of speech the petitions which ought to be made to God in a restrained way. God listens, not to the voice, but to the heart, and since he reads our thoughts, He does not need to have His attention called by clamour" (St. Cyprian: *On the Lord's Prayer*, Breviary No. 111, pp. 188-189).

St. Catherine of Siena – Perfect prayer is not attained through many words, but through affection of desire ... (Dialogue: pp. 166).

Catherine Doherty – Prayer does not need words" (Poustinia: p. 75).

**The stories will make the point clear:**

(i) Sometimes some people pray like the prophets of Baal. "Answer us Baal" (see 1 Kg. 18:27-39). But Baal did not answer them. Elijah prayed. God flashed out. It is good to read this story from 1 Kg. 18:27-39.

(ii) St. Augustine's experiences too is important here. He says: "When shall I set down the record of those days of rest? One thing at least I shall not fail to tell, for I have not forgotten the sting of your lash nor how quickly your mercy came, and in how wonderful a way. During that vacation you let me suffer the agony of toothache, and when the pain became so great that I could not speak, my heart prompted me to ask all my friends who were with me to pray to you for me, since you are the God who gives health to the body as well as to the soul. I wrote down the message and gave it to them to read, and as soon as we knelt down to offer you this humble prayer, the pain vanished. What was that pain? How did it vanish? My Lord and my God, I confess that I was terrified, for nothing like this had ever happened to me in all my life. Deep within me I recognised the working of your will and I praised your name, rejoicing in my faith" (Confessions, p. 189).

Somebody says: "In this matter of prayer more is obtained by signs than by speech, more by tears than by words" (Brev. III p. 256). We saw the truth in the manner Hanna prayed. She won God's favours through her insistent, silent, prayer (1 Sam. 1:18-22).

(3) **What is most important to pray for?**

The first thing to pray for should be an increase of faith, hope and charity – the theological virtues. Please read Lk. 11:1-13. Seek first the Kingdom of God and every other thing will follow in the way it will rebound to the glory of God and your Salvation (Lk. 12:31). He who has God, has all that is necessary for life and salvation.

(4) **There is need to listen while you pray:**

Prayer is a dialogue, a communion. It ceases to be so if the only voice heard is that of the one who prays. We should listen to the Lord while we pray (Eccl. 6:33). If you are willing to listen, you will learn how to pray well.

(5) **Make yourself clean and forgive others:**

Isaiah 59:1-5 told his people: "Don't think that the Lord is too weak to save you or too deaf to hear you call for help. It is because of your sins that he doesn't hear you. It is your sins that separate you from God when you come to worship him. You are guilty of lying, violence and murder". And when the people of Judah and Jerusalem went on with their sin of idolatry (sacrificing to Baal), the Lord said to Jeremiah that when the people would cry to him for help, He would not *listen* to them. He in fact told Jeremiah himself, "don't pray to me or plead with me for help, I will not listen to them" (Jer. 11:11-14; 7:1-15).

So prayer that works and holy life are connected. Sin can be a barrier. And so we hear our Lord and Master tell us in the gospel: "And when you stand and pray, forgive anything you may have against anyone, so that your Father in heaven will forgive the wrongs you have done" (Mk. 11:25).

(6) **Pray as a group (the family should do this):**

We are told that a family that prays together, stays together. Individuals should of course, pray in their privacy but *there is power in united prayer*. This is the teaching of the Lord. "If two of you join your voices on earth to pray for anything whatever, it shall be granted you by my Father in heaven" (Matt. 18:19-20). That is, if you pray for good things.

(7) **Pray with the spirit of submission and humility:**

The word of God teaches us to pray with *faith* and in *full assurance* (Mt. 21:22; James 1:6; Heb. 10:22), confidence in God (Ps. 56:9; 86:7; 1 Jn. 5:14). And even with boldness (Heb.

4:16), but we must be humble to submit our prayers to the Lord's will. He Himself ended His prayer at the garden of Gethsemane in the spirit of surrender: "Not what I want but what you want" (Mt. 26:39). This is true prayer; a prayer of one who has faith in the Father's providential care. "Faith that is firm is also patient", says the Lord (Is. 28:16).

(8) **Don't put the Lord to test:**
The Lord has great power. His arms are not short to save. However, it is a principle in theology that God does not accomplish by a miracle what can be done in the ordinary way by secondary causes. For example, someone about to travel, providentially discovers that the brakes are not functioning well, he ignores this, hoping on God's protection from harm. The ability to see that the brakes are not in good order is the Lord's work. The same with those who get ill and refuse to submit to the doctor. Please read Sirach 38:1-15. God created both Doctor and medicine, so says Scripture. DO NOT PUT THE LORD TO TEST.

(9) **Pray and wait:** (Ps. 40:1)
Edward Farrell in his book "Surprised by the Spirit", tells the story of asking a hermit (Brother John) on Cat Island in the Bahamas, to give him a 'word'. The man of God did not say anything for the four days or five that Farrell was there. When Farrell was leaving, the hermit said to him:

"When you go back and talk with your people tell them to be patient with God, to wait for Him". ("As Bread That is Broken" p. 38 by Peter G. Van Breemon, S.J.)

Julian of Norwich has a very consoling thought in one of her writings. She says:

"Sometimes it seems to us that we have been praying a long time, and yet nothing seems to happen. We do not see any answer. We should not get despondent (lose hope) about this. I believe our Lord intends by this either that we should await a more suitable time, or more grace or a better gift".

(10) God loves to answer our prayers because by this, His glory is revealed (Jn. 14:13).

# Q. 51 Should a Catholic Christian take part in traditional religious beliefs and practices?

(1) What the people in other religions are looking for, we have already. All human searches for God are fulfilled in Christ; God's secret Wisdom, hidden for centuries for mankind,

now revealed to us who are chosen by God for His glory (1 Cor. 2:7-10).

(a) He himself said that He is the Truth, the Way and the Life (Jn. 14:6).

(b) Paul says: "He is God's yes; for it is he who is the YES to all of God's promises. This is why through Jesus Christ our "AMEN" is said to the glory of God" (2 Cor. 1:19-22).

(c) John the Beloved says that in Christ Jesus we have the endless accumulation of God's blessings (Jn. 1:16) (Grace upon grace – fullness of blessings). What are those blessings:

    (i) Immortal (undying) and glorious life; an everlasting life with God.

    (ii) Truth – We now know the mind of God towards us. The author of the letter to the Hebrews sais that God, in many and different ways, spoke to our ancestors, but now He has spoken to us CLEARLY in His Son (Heb. 1:1ff). We are no longer in the dark. The Bible says the Light has come (Is. 9:1-7; Titus 2:11-14; Jn. 3:19; 9:5).

(2) Redemption – No one is any longer a victim of sin, and Satan. There is salvation available for whoever cares to come to Christ and stay with Him. Outside Him, there is trouble. In Him we are saved.

Given all these, we have no need of any other god or any other religion. We have all we need to be saved from sin, and Satanic influences. "God's grace has been revealed and it has made Salvation possible for the whole human race" (Titus 2:11ff). 2 Pt. 1:1-3 – says God has given us all we need to live a truly religious life, great and precious gifts so that by means of these gifts we might escape the destructive lust that is in the world and may come to share the divine nature".

(3) **What are the people in traditional religion doing?**

In our introduction to this Question, we pointed out that people in traditional religion are searching for what we have. They are searching for grace and truth – God and Salvation. They are ignorant of how they can be saved from sin and Satanic powers, and so they resort to magic, talisman and all other kinds of charms, animal sacrifices in order to avert misfortune; they slaughter animals and sprinkle the blood on their carved idols so as to gain forgiveness of sins. They spend a lot to appease their gods. The Bible tells them "You are Wrong". The letter to the Hebrews tells us that through Jesus, the believer is saved from SIN, FEAR and DEATH; and Jesus as the High Priest, provides the true Salvation, which was only foreshadowed by the rituals and animal sacrifices of the Hebrew religion (Heb. 10:1-18). "The blood of goats and bulls can never take away sins" (Heb. 10:4).

(4) **Are we condemning Traditional Religious beliefs, practices and forms of worship?**

We are not condemning their religion whole and entire. There are some elements of truth in what they say and do. Whenever Jesus heard people say the truth or do what is right, He praised it. An example will make the point clear.

(a) Jesus praised the faith of a pagan (a centurion) (Lk. 7:9): "I have never found so much faith in Israel". The Christian is free to imitate the strong faith of the pagans. Jesus took some of the customs of His people. For example:

(b) He used mud and saliva to heal a blind man (Jn. 9:6). We are told that the ancient used spittle from a fasting person to heal.

If we find any good in the traditional religion, we should take it, for truth does not contradict truth. Whatever is good is from God, and so, if we find anything good in traditional religious beliefs and practices, we should take it after careful examination. Let us take, as a case, the African traditional way of praying; their way of worship. By traditional Africa here I mean Africans in West, Central and East Africa who still hold to the religion of our ancestors. We observe that the common characteristics of their worship is the wonderful dynamism and joyfulness that one rarely finds in some Christian worship. Experts have pointed out that the traditional African prayer can be described as a 'charismatic improvisation' for the needs of the moment. It is spontaneous; it is a personal expression of one's feeling in the community to God. There is certainly some value of Catholicism here and that is, that aspect of the charismatic improvisation, spontaneity, joy in their worship and a sharing of experiences. Christian religious communities in Africa should take an example from traditional religion. They should not be afraid to share experiences. We are so shy to share deep spiritual need and experiences. We should share experiences; for sharing in this way, the Church becomes a power-house, a place for the renewal of faith.

(5) Unfortunately, some Christian communities still pray with dry faces as if the Christian life is a tragedy. "Rejoice in the Lord always; again I will say, Rejoice". That is the voice of Paul to the Christians of Philippi – Phil. 4:4. We should pray spontaneously, rejoice in the Lord. People in other religions do not have more hope of a better life than us.

(6) **How are the people in Traditional Religion trapping the Christians and getting them to become their members?**

They do not go about preaching, trying to win converts as we Christians do. They simply use very subtle, dangerous methods to entice people into membership of their religion in the following ways:

(i) By the offer of political power.

Christians complain that if they don't take religious titles, they will not have a say in the affairs of the Society. "In the gathering of the people, you will not be allowed to speak". So to have the power to speak, one enters into the cult of elders.

(ii) They use all forms of social pressure.

(iii) Rejection (Ostracism).

(7) Funeral ceremonies are the test-cases. Here the problem shows clearly. Among some ethnic groups when a woman dies, her body is to be carried to her family for burial. And for most of our people still practising the religion of our ancestors, it does not matter whether the woman is a Christian or not – all they want is their daughter's remains. At the funeral, the children of the woman (it does not matter to them whether they are Christians or not) should perform the funeral according to the norms of the traditional religion. If you refuse to do whatever they say, the deceased (dead) woman will have a controversial, disgraceful funeral. There are very few Catholics who will be prepared to carry such a cross.

(8) Again, when a man dies (it does not matter whether the man was a Christian or not), his wife and children will be subjected to the traditional form of burial. In some towns in Bendel, the woman is forced to weep over and over again. She should dress up in dirty clothes and sit on the floor. She will be confined to the house for days or months. She will not go to the Church. If she dies in that condition, she is an abomination. Her funeral will be one of sorrow.

(9) **What if a Christian man or woman were to have the courage to protest: "I will not do what you ask me to do?"**

Such a Christian will face several consequences and many Christians are not ready to go through this kind of suffering. The psychological – social wars the Christian will face are again:

(a) **Rejection:** The people will persuade others to reject you – nobody will enter your house again. You don't have to greet people; and nobody should greet you. Whoever visits you, or greets you or eats with you, will himself or herself come under the interdict and the curse. Unfortunately, some Christians will join with the persecutors and disown you. Some Catholics even persuade their fellow Catholics to compromise – to agree with the pagans.

(b) *Curse:* It is also believed that whoever disregards the beliefs and practices of the people is automatically under a curse – He or she will soon meet with a disaster, for the deceased ancestors, the divinities (gods) and the ruling elders will be angered and it is terrible to incur the displeasure of these powers. Faithless Christians over and over again succumb to this kind of threat. But the truth is that the dead ancestors have no power to harm anybody; they themselves, if they are not in heaven, are looking for help from us (we believe in praying for the dead).

We should bear in mind that the gods of these people are pure Creation of the People – "Ogunpa", "Oloku", "Idigu", "Mkpitime", "Oshun", are human-made gods – deified matters. The Bible teaches us that there is no other god but the Lord. And those who believe in these nature gods are doing harm to themselves. Two times, the Psalmist prays that those who made idols and believe in them "become like the idols they have made" (Ps. 115:8; 135:15-18).

(c) They also make use of threats such as:

You are responsible for the evil that may happen from then on to the entire area: Because you disobey, the people will hand over life and property in the area to your care. If any evil happens to the people, you will be held responsible. It is believed that disobedience is responsible for moral disorder or any evil that happens in human society.

(d) The pressure from your immediate relations:

Your relations who are not Christians will put pressure on you to obey the people. They will argue that if you don't do what they ask you to do, your entire family will be in for it. Sometimes you may not be willing to listen to others outside one's family but it is difficult for one to reject the views of one's own blood relations.

(e) Divided loyalty among Christians:

When all these are happening, the greatest shock you are likely to get is from your fellow Christians. They will disown you and call your names.

One thing that is not clear:

(i) When a non-Christian dies, Christians don't go to ask for the body in order to perform Christian rituals but when a Christian dies, the non-Christians want the body of the Christian; they want to bury the Christian in their own way (according to their own rites). The curious question is why?

(ii) Why should a baptized deceased Christian be subject to non-Christian funeral rite?

Bearing in mind all that happens at such funerals, we should remind ourselves again that the Sovereign Lord condemned pagan worship:

My people, the Lord says, are asking for "revelation from a piece of wood! A stick tells them what they want to know!

They have left me. Like a woman who becomes a prostitute, they have given themselves to other gods . . . The people of Israel are under the spell of idols . . . They will be carried away as by the wind, and they will be ashamed of their pagan sacrifices" (Hosea 4:11-19).

## There should be no compromise

"Come out from among them . . ." (2 Cor. 6:14-18).

We must be obstinate. We should not yield. We should not compromise. We should decide either in favour of Christian life and funeral or pagan life and funeral. It is either or. Look at the life of Christ. Christ did not compromise.

(i) He did not forget His identity and mission.

(ii) He was not caught in the net of the political philosophies of the Zealots (violence), not discouraged by the attitude of the members of the Sanhedrin or any other group of opposition (Jn. 7:48; 11-13). He held to the will of God (Jn. 4:34).

(iii) He was not discouraged by the opposition of sinners (Heb. 12:3).

The Bible encourages us to do the same – to keep firm. The book of Hebrews reminds us that in our fight against sin (it is a sin to sell one's conscience to the pagans), we have not yet resisted to the point of shedding blood (Heb. 12:4). What is demanded of us is simply to be prepared to be rejected. A woman says: "they will ostracise my children". There is glory in suffering for Christ's sake (1 Pt. 2:18-24). Social pressures and rejection is all that is involved. We will only be given names – fool, madman, a threat to society, but these are the names that people have always given to those who change the process of history, prophets who listen to God, who do the will of God, and announce the same to their societies.

Resist all kinds of tricks, deceitful, political manoeuvres. Remember the story of Polycarp (c. 23 Feb. 155 – Bishop of Smyrna). He chose Christ as His Lord. This choice angered the Governor of his country. He was earmarked to be killed. And this was how he was arrested:

(1) **Commissioner of Police** – "Come now, where is the harm in saying: "Caesar is Lord" and offering the incense, and so forth, when it will save your life?"
    **Polycarp** – "No, I am not going to take your advice". (As Polycarp stepped into the arena, there came a voice from heaven, "Be strong, Polycarp, and play the man". No one caught sight of the speaker . . .").

(2) **The Governor** – "Have respect for your years. Swear an oath "By the Luck of Caesar". "Take the oath and I will let you go".

(3) **Polycarp** – Eighty-six years I have served Him and He has done me no wrong. How then can I blaspheme my King and my Saviour?" Polycarp was stabbed to death (Early Christian Writings, pp. 159-161).

### SUMMARY

**What was the offence of Polycarp?**
 (i) He refused to say "Caesar is Lord"
(ii) He refused to offer incense to the Emperor's guardian spirit.

**Accusation:**
He was called "the man who destroys our gods".
We must imitate Polycarp. Our mission is to destroy false gods and all the beliefs and practices they encourage.
**PRAYER:** Eph. 3:16-20.

# Q. 52  What does the Bible say about the evil in the world?

(1) In the Bible, we are told that God created man for happiness (Gn. 2:5-25), but sickness and all other sufferings came into the world as a result of sin (Gen. 3:16-19). Eve would have trouble in pregnancy while giving birth. The man, Adam, would have to struggle to live – this was the loss of paradise, following God's judgment. So evil is there in the world because man sinned. Again the presence of misfortune, particularly sickness was in the Old Testament conception, considered as a blow from the God of justice (Ex. 4:6; Job. 16:12ff; Ps; 39:11) (Xavier Leon-Dufour "Suffering" Dict. of Biblical Theology, pp. 587-590).

"You punish a man's sins by your rebukes, and like a moth you destroy what he loves".

This is a religious interpretation of human suffering, particularly in a culture that sees events in the world from the angle of religion. We shall make reference to the persistence of this thinking in the analysis of the suffering of Job.

The Old Testament puts up two possible solutions to the mystery of evil in the world: Suffering is a test. Put differently:

(a) "This suffering of a just man is a providential test to show whether his faith in the Lord is genuine (See Judges 8:21-23). The New Testament authors take up this view (See 1 Pet. 1:6-7; James 1:2-4).

(b) The suffering of the sinner is a punishment for his evil deeds.

(2) Genesis' View as to why there is evil:

Man's original state was one of innocence (Gn. 2:25) and friendship with God (Gn. 3:8). Man sinned and the effect is the common lot of all his descendants. This sin resulted in a whole trail of disaster. Jerome Biblical commentary lined them up thus:

(a) Loss of divine friendship (Gn. 3:23-24).

(b) Lack of mutual esteem (Gn. 3:7).

(c) Physical evils in accord with the nature of man (Gn. 3:17-19) and of woman (Gn. 3:16).

(d) Constant struggle against the power of evil (Gn. 3:15).

But the promise of ultimate victory in the struggle (Gn. 3:15b) is given by the God whose saving will was manifested so clearly in Israel's regard. The continuing struggle resulted at first in continuing defeat for man (Gn. 4:1-16). Murder (Gn. 4:1-8), vengeance (Gn. 4:24), polygamy (Gn. 4:19) and concupiscence of the flesh (Gn. 6:5); all these awful events marked the history of man and of civilisation (Gn. 4:17-22). The offended divine justice is expressed in the natural catastrophes that overtook man (Gn. 6:6-7; 11-13); his mercy and will to save is expressed in the salvation of the just (Gn. 6:8-9). But God's covenant with the just man, symbolized in nature (Gn. 9:8-17), was followed by men continuing to do evil (Gn. 9:20-27), which resulted in the alienation of human society from God and of men from one another (Gn. 11:1-9). (Eugene H. Maly, "Genesis" in Jerome Biblical Commentary, p. 9)

**Summary of Genesis position:**

In the Old Testament conception, everything was fine at the beginning of creation; the first fall triggered a moral disorder and the consequences that follow. The author of the book of Genesis tells us that God made all things and saw that it was good (Gn. 1:1-2; 25). In Gn. 3:1-24, we see the beginning of sin and suffering. Cain killed Abel. Seeing his punishment he got frightend and cried out:

"This punishment (punishment due to his sin) is too hard for me to bear" (Gn. 4:13).

After this, wickedness spread among mankind (Gn. 6:1ff). The greatest evil resulting from sin was death. Wisdom 1:12-16, says that even death is not God's making. Death came because of sin. Moral evil led the Supreme God to permit that men and their evils be wiped away by the flood (Gn. 7:1-8; 8:22).

(3) **Peculiarities of the Old Testament conception of the problem of evil**

    (i) Dufour says: the "O.T. is not familiar with the idea of voluntary suffering in the ascetic and Pauline sense" (p. 587).

  (ii) They also believe that "wounds can be produced by natural agents (Gn. 34:25; Joshua 5:8, 2 Sam. 4:4) and infirmities of old age are normal" (Gn. 27:1; 48:10) (p. 587).

 (iii) The common belief though is that there are "evil powers in the universe hostile to man, those of the curse are of satan. Sin brings misery (Prov. 13:8; Is. 3:11; Sir. 7:1) and there is a tendency to look for a fault at the source of every woe (Gn. 12:17; 42:21; Joshua 7:6-13).

This is the conviction of the friends of Job. At the source of the evil which weighs upon the world, there must be placed the first sin (Gn. 3:14-19).

(4) **The problem of evil creates two scandals:**

    (i) The prophets cannot understand the prosperity of the wicked and

  (ii) The misery of the just (Jeremiah 12:1-6; Habbakuk 1:13). The just when persecuted believe that they must be forgotten (Ps. 13:2; 31:13; 44:10-18). And so we see Job enter into an accusation against God and he summons him to explain himself (Job. 13:22; 23:7).

(5) **Job and the problem of evil**

The book of Job is the story of a good man who suffers total disaster. He loses all his children and property and is afflicted with a repulsive disease. Job and his friends reacted to these calamities. The friends of Job explained Job's sufferings in traditional religious terms (the one constant thing in the attitude of the Old Testament people was that they had a religious interpretation of events in the world).

Job's friends believed, as the rest of the people did believe, that God always rewards good and punishes evil; so, the sufferings of Job can only mean that he has sinned.

What was Job's reaction to the fact – the evil that came upon him? According to Job, the arguments of his friends that he sinned is too simple; he does not believe that he deserved such cruel punishment because he had been an unusually good and righteous man. He could not understand how God could let much evil happen to one like himself and he boldly challenged God:

"Why let me go on living in misery? ... They wait for death, but it never comes; ... I have no peace, no rest, and my troubles never end" (Job. 3:20-26).

To his friends, Job said:

"If my troubles and griefs were weighed on scales, they would weigh more than the sands of the sea, so my wild words should not surprise you. Almighty God has shot me with arrows ..." (Job. 6:1-4).

Job does not lose his faith, but he wants to be justified before God and to regain his honour as a good man. Since the Hebrew believed that the one who experiences evil – sickness and misfortunes of all kinds – must have done some evil, it was proper that Job longed to be justified. In the New Testament, we see this belief persisting: The disciples of Jesus once asked him when they saw a blind man: "Teacher, whose sin caused him to be born blind? Was it his own or his parents' sin"? (Jn. 9:1-2). This question was asked because, "Among the Jews it was a common belief that all misfortunes were a result of sins committed either by the unfortunate person or by his parents" (Commentary on Jn. 9:2 by the Confraternity of Christian Doctrine Bible). As an objection to the belief of the Old Testament Jews, the Confraternity Bible says:

"This is not always true, although it is true in many cases. God sometimes permits the innocent to suffer for his own particular ends" (p. 412).

The problem of evil in the Old Testament is therefore, linked with the mystery of sin. Job claimed that he was not a sinner (Job. 33:9-13) but when he came to a fresh view of God, he humbly acknowledged God as wise and great and repented of the will and angry words he had used:

"In the past I knew only what others had told me, but now I have seen you with my own eyes. So I am ashamed of all I have said and repent in dust and ashes" (Job 42:5-6).

In the end, God won over the afflicted Job.

106

(6) **God and the renewed world:**
Evil alienated man from God. We are told that the tower of Babel stands as a symbol of man's prideful rebellion. Man had tried to achieve a state beyond his created nature and that was his sin (Gn. 3:1-6). The sin led to disunity among humans. Pentecost event (Acts 2:5-12) would usher in a new era of peace and unity. But the effect of man's turning away from his God is man's alienation from the source of his being and the alienation of "men from one another". The prophets would announce the future reversal of this movement (cf. Is. 2:1-5), and as has been pointed out, their prophecies were fulfilled on the day the Holy Spirit was sent on the apostles in the city of Jerusalem. God is not defeated by man's evil deeds. The world was messed up but God started all over again to put things right – to recreate the human person badly injured by sin and sickness. This is the theology of the St. Mark's gospel – God has come to recreate the wounded world. The Bible consolation is that God can triumph.

(7) **God has power over evil**
The story of Joseph and his brothers (Gn. 37:1ff) points out the fact that evil cannot destroy God's plan. He has power to bring good out of evil. God is not a slave of situations. He is Lord and Master of all situations; He is the Lord of history.

Because God has power to bring good out of evil, "suffering has an intercessory and redemptive value. This value appears in the figure of Moses, in his sorrowful prayer (Exodus 17:11ff; Number 11:1ff), and in the sacrifice of his life, which he offers to save a guilty people" (Exodus 32:30-33). (Dufour, p. 588).

(8) **How should man respond to the reality of evil?**
According to the Old Testament, man's salvation (freedom from sin, sickness, satan and death) is in the hand of the Sovereign Lord. Man plagued by evil has to do the following:

(a) Follow the commandments (Dt. 11:26-28):
"Today I am giving you the choice between a blessing and a curse – A BLESSING if you obey . . . a curse if you disobey".

(b) Trust the Lord (Ps. 46:10):
"Be still and know that I am God". The Sovieregn Lord is the people's Shepherd. "Even if I go through the deepest darkness, I will not be afraid, Lord, for you are with me" (Ps. 23:4).

(c) Pray to be Saved:
In the Old Testament belief, prayer has power to change evil situations (See Jews and Amalekites' fight Ex.

17:11-13) and the evils to come hence the Psalmist says:
So all your loyal people should pray to you in times of need;
when a great flood of trouble comes rushing in, it will not
reach them" (Ps. 32:6).

In moments of trial, man should trust God for a "person
cannot redeem himself" (Ps. 49:7). God is the one who saves.

## (9) The judgment of evil that men do in the world

In the Old Testament, faith in the judgment of God is
never in doubt. God is the ruler of the world. He knows the
hearts and minds of men (Jeremiah 11:20; 17:10). He knows
perfectly the just and sinners. Since He dominates events,
he cannot fail to shape them in such a way that in the end,
the just will escape from their trials and the wicked will be
punished. That there is an eschatological judgment
(eschatology deals with the final events, death, judgment,
heaven and hell), is an idea which underlies all the
prophecies of punishment (ch. Is. 1:24ff; 5:5ff). From Amos
on, the Bible transforms the day of the Lord by adding an
element of terror (Amos 5:18ff). Israel, the unfaithful spouse,
will be judged according to the law applying to adulterers
(Ez. 16:38; 23:24) and her sons will be judged according to
their behaviour and their words (Ez. 36:19)(Dufour, p. 278).

Retribution in Psalms and Job is one of the key themes
which run through much of the Old Testament. This Hebrew
belief seems to have been based on their concept of God as
just and powerful. His justice demanded the reward of the
good and the punishment of the wicked, while his power was
such that his justice could not be frustrated.

The early stage of this retribution showed that it was
"something collective and temporal" (Albert Gelin). And
this concept of collective responsibility both for sins
committed and the punishment due, was based on the
solidarity of the group in action. Ezekiel 18:30 would change
the idea of solidarity in sin and punishment: the one who
does evil is the one to die. There was the idea of temporal
and individual punishment. The other-wordly (in another
world) retribution became explicit in Wisdom. The soul of
the virtuous is in the hand of the Lord (Ws. 3:1ff).

## The Bible says that Evil will End (Rev. 21:1-5)

The Old Testament does not believe that they were trapped.
There were signs of hope. Isaiah had predicted God's victory and
man's eternal happiness:
"Here on Mount Zion the Lord Almighty will prepare a
banquet for all nations of the world – a banquet of the richest
food and finest wine. Here he will suddenly remove the cloud

of sorrow that has been hanging over all the nations. The Sovereign Lord will destroy death forever! He will wipe away the tears from everyone's eyes and take away the disgrace his people have suffered throughout the world" (Is. 25:6-9).

This is theology of the future. Man's ultimate destiny is victory and happiness. The New Testament would tell us that this victory and establishment of a new age has been inaugurated in the appearance of God-in-Christ. The New American Bible commenting on Romans 8:31-39, says:

"The all conquering power of God's love has overcome every obstacle to man's salvation and every threat of his separation from God. That power was manifested fully when God delivered up to death even his own Son for our Salvation. Through him, the Christian can overcome all his afflictions and trials".

### What should be man's attitude towards evils that come upon him?

The Old Testament realizes the smallness, the weakness and the dignity of man: "what is man, that you think of him; *mere* man, that you care for him?" (Ps. 8:4); it points out therefore, that only in total submission to the Sovereign Lord is man saved when a flood of disaster comes upon him. In quietness and trust lies man's salvation (Is. 7:9). Recall the trials of Job. His reaction to the first trial (Job 1:13-19) has been echoed by many saints and considered as a classical expression of virtuous resignation to the will of God: "The Lord gave and the Lord has taken away; blessed be the name of the Lord" (Job 1:21). In a similar way, by his response to the second trial (Job 2:1-10) Job shows that he has passed through the temptations without sin. Kissane sums up the effect of this first portion of the book:

"The author's purpose is achieved; Job's innocence is beyond question; it is recognised by God; admitted by the Satan and expressly stated by the writer himself at the conclusion of each of Job's trials" (Edward J. Kissane, *The Book of Job*, p. 10).

The last point (certainly not the least significant): The presence of evil is an enigma when we consider the power of the living God – consider His incomparable attributes: omnipotence, wisdom and love. How do we reconcile the existence of this all-powerful God of love and the reality of evil? The constant question is: If God is powerful, why has He not wiped out evil? The question of human freedom solves a little of the problem. The Old Testament authors and people do not ask all these questions. Their view being simply: evil came into existence as a result of sin. Even physical disasters have their root in the cosmic disorder created by the first fall.

The question is: how far can we accept the Bible's interpretation of human tragedy as we find? It depends on what one thinks about the world as a whole – its origin, nature and purpose. In the Old Testament thought, God made all things and they were good (Genesis theology); the evil we now find, is not God's doing; it is the work of Sin.

# Q. 53 Is worship due to angels and saints?

At one of our prayer meetings, a brother in the Lord read a passage of the Holy Scripture (Colossians 2:16-19) and one other brother commented shortly on the reading. His interpretation was controversial.

Paul, in the passage in question was trying to make the Colossian Christians realise the sovereign role of Christ, for the people were worried about 'spirits' that were controlling them. They were also worried about rules regarding food and drink. Paul told the people that all such beliefs were human "precepts and doctrines". He, Paul, was not telling the people not to have anything to do with the Angels of God. The good Angels are still our friends, as the Bible would show.

Now I would like to aks the question: Do we adore or worship Angels and Saints?

(1) What does the word worship mean? To worship means to pay the highest honour to a divine being. At the lenten period, we say to the Crucified Christ: We adore you O Christ because by your holy Cross you have redeemed the world. We do not use the word adore or worship when we are dealing with the angels or saints; rather, we use the word VENERATE, which of course, means to look upon with respect and admiration.

(2) The Catholic Church teaches that "It is forbidden to give divine honour or worship to the Angels and saints, for this belongs to God alone". This is forbidden beause God alone is Creator – He is the Creator of heaven and earth. He made us. He is keeping us alive. He is the one working out our salvation – who will bring us to heaven. And so, to Him alone shall we pay the HIGHEST HONOUR. The Angel told John: "WORSHIP GOD ALONE" (Rev. 19:10).

(3) We however, should admire and give respect to the good Angels and saints, for this is due to them as the servants and special friends of God. We are even asked by the Bible to look at the lives of those who have gone ahead of us and to follow their example. Let us listen to the voice of Scripture: "REMEMBER YOUR LEADERS WHO SPOKE THE WORD OF GOD TO YOU: *CONSIDER* HOW THEIR LIVES

ENDED AND IMITATE THEIR FAITH" (Heb. 13:7-8). Even while still alive, Paul told the Christians at Corinth: "IMITATE ME AS I IMITATE CHRIST" (1 Cor. 11:1). To the Philippians, he also said: "BE IMITATORS OF ME, BROTHERS"; follow my example (Phil. 3:17; 4:9); Example is the best teacher.

(B) Why do we venerate the angels and saints and ask them to pray for us?

    (i) The Catholic Church teaches us that "WE SHOULD ASK THE ANGELS AND SAINTS TO PRAY FOR US, BECAUSE THEY ARE YOUR FRIENDS AND BRETHREN, AND BECAUSE THEIR PRAYERS HAVE GREAT POWER WITH GOD". The Angels and Saints are with us in our struggles to live well and get back to God. The Lord said that even there IS JOY BEFORE THE ANGELS OF GOD UPON ONE SINNER DOING PENANCE" (Lk. 15:10).

In this life, we pray for one another; we ask for one another's prayers. Paul, over and over again, prayed for people and asked them to pray for him (2 Tim. 1:3; Eph. 6:18-20, pray that God may put His words on my lips, that I may courageously make known the mystery of the gospel). "If we can pray for one another in this life, why can we not continue to do so after death?" (See Question 6a).

# Q. 54 Should a Catholic Christian join secret societies?

What is a Secret Society?

"A Secret Society means a society or association, not being a solely cultural or religious body that uses Secret Signs, Oaths, Rites or Symbols –

(1) Whose meetings or other activities are held in secret.

(2) Whose members are under Oath, Obligation or other threat to promote the interest of its members or to aid one another under all circumstances without due regard to merit, fair play or justice, to the detriment of the legitimate expectation of those who are not members" (Federal Nigerian Constitution: Ch. IV, "Fundamental Rights", No. 35 (4)).

The problem with Secret Societies is not because their meetings are held in secret but because they carry on activities which are against the principles of love and justice. As the Federal Nigerian Government Constitution sees them, members of such Societies take an oath to promote the interests of their members without due regard to merit, fair play or justice. An example will make the point clear: If you are a member of a

111

Secret Cult and you stole something from your employer, and you are charged to the court where the Judge, who is also a member of your Secret Cult is to preside over the case, all of a sudden, the Judge says that you did not steal, even though he is aware that you did steal something from your employer, such a judgment is a perversion of justice. The Judge has acted without due regard to justice. The only reason why you were set free from the just demands of the law that prohibits stealing is because you belong to a secret society in which the Judge who tried your case is a member.

In the old Code of Canon Law (c. 2335), the Catholic Church understands Secret Societies to be associations which truly plot against the Church. All plots against the Church will usually originate in a Secret meeting by the plotters, hence it will be right to consider such anti-Catholic Organisations as a "Secret Society".

Why do members of Secret Societies hold their meetings in secret? The reason is because they practice evil. The Bible says that he who practises evil hates the light; he does not come near it for fear his deeds will be exposed" (John: 3:20-21).

Since members of Secret Societies destroy the course of fair play and justice, they come under the judgment of the Bible (Is. 5:20-23).

It is the love of the glory of this life that leads men into "Secret Societies". The warning of the Sovereign Lord is:

"What will it profit a man to gain the whole world and suffer the loss of his own soul"? (Matt. 16:26).

"Secret Societies" are engaged in works of darkness. The Bible warns us not to take part in worthless, "vain deeds done in darkness" (Eph. 5:11-12). It also says that "Bad men all hate the light and avoid it, for fear their practices should be shown up. The honest man comes to the light so that it may be clearly seen that God is in all he does" (John 3:20).

He who joins a Secret Society has joined the society of agents of darkness. The plain truth is that he who walks in the dark does not know where he is going.

## Q. 55 What is the best gift we ought to give to God?

Read Lk. 18:18-30, there are few things the Bible asks us to do in order that we might be pleasing to our God. Some of them seem very easy and some are not. For example: It is easy to give some kobo to a beggar and even give a lot of money to him but it is never too easy to bring the beggar to your house and eat at the same table with him.

Again it is easy to fast from morning to evening, on your own free decision but it is not all that easy for you to take an insult or a slap from someone you know you could very well handle without exerting your energy or resources.

Again it appears easy to keep the commandments but it is not so easy to give oneself and one's possessions to God. The rich man in the gospel (Lk. 18:18-30) proves the point. He kept the commandments but was not prepared to do more for the Lord. What he was saying in effect to the Lord is: I OWN MYSELF AND MY POSSESSIONS AND I LOVE ALL OF THEM; I CANNOT SURRENDER THEM TO YOU. I AM ALL RIGHT KEEPING THE COMMANDMENTS WHICH YOU GAVE US. But was he wrong in keeping the commandments? Of course not! Why was he wrong? The answer is precisely because there are duties which we owe to the Lord: Keeping the commandments and surrendering to Him.

We have to build up ourselves in the Lord. In short, we have been saved, we should do all we can to remain a saved people. This calls for keeping the commandments and practising the virtues. The Lord told us: "If you love me keep the commandments". So the rich man in the gospel was not doing something wrong by keeping the commandments.

The Good News however, teaches us that the following of Christ calls for self sacrifice and complete self-giving (total dedication). If you read St. Paul, he is equally clear that the response to the gospel will involve a life of dedicated toughness. It will be costly. Men must make sacrifices.

If we are convinced of who the Lord is to us, we wouldn't count the cost of following Him. Love does not count the cost of loving. Abraham proved to God that he loved Him when he was prepared to give God his best gift, what he loved most in life, namely ISAAC. Hannah gave the Lord her only Son in gratitude to what God did for her. Those Old Testament personalities were truly in love with God – they were detached from the gifts of God and were attached to the will of God.

Some people claim that they love God, but they love God because their interest is involved. An example, if God has power to protect me and my dearest ones, then it is good to love God and if obeying His commandments means that I will go to heaven, then it is good to obey God's commandments. All such reasons for loving God and keeping His commandments may be good but they are not pure love of God. They are selfish.

The N.T. teaches us that there is more to believing in God than keeping the commandments. Lk. 18:18-30 says that a man of great wealth had wanted to know what he could do to have life everlasting . . . But he went away sad. Though he knew the commandments and kept them, but that was not enough. Remember that he loved heaven and loved his riches but he could not do away with his riches to have greater ones in heaven. He was perhaps, working on the principle: What you have, you hold.

St. Augustine says: A man loves God less if he loves something more than God Himself. Take the case of the rich man:

Certainly, that man loved his riches more than God, for when the Lord said to Him: Follow me, he was said to have preferred created things to His Creator. What was wrong with him? He was so deeply in love with what he owned that he could not respond to God's offer of life everlasting. Where your treasure is, there your heart will be. Whatever a person loves most is his God.

THE BEST GIFT IS: Oneself. Seneca relates that a certain disciple of Socrates, Aeschines, not being able to repay Socrates on account of his poverty, as his fellow disciples did, went out and said to him: "Master, extreme poverty leaves me nothing to give you something as a token of my gratitude, I offer you, then, myself, to be yours forever".

"Truly", said Socrates, "you have given me more than all the rest"

No one gives as much as the one who gives himself and all that he or she owns to the Lord.

Have you ever thought about Lk. 19:11-27?

Reflect on it.

# Q. 56 What is the difference between the sacrament of Confirmation and Baptism in the Holy Spirit?

(1) What does Confirmation mean?

It is the sacrament which gives us special help to live a good Christian life. When you have received the Holy Spirit in Confirmation, you do not fear or feel ashamed to talk about Jesus because by the gift of the Holy Spirit, you are made strong and powerful (Acts 4:8, 31: 5:32; 6:10; Phil. 1:19).

(2) What is it necessary to be confirmed?

It is necessary because through the sacrament of confirmation, you will receive power from God to be witnesses of the Good News for Jesus Himself promised us this when He said:

"And now I am sending down to you what the Father has promised. Stay in the city then, until you are clothed with the power from on high (Lk. 24:49; Acts 1:8).

(3) Who sent the Holy Spirit on the first Christians – the Apostles?

Jesus promised that when he got to heaven, he would send the Holy Spirit to help the Church in bearing witness to the Good News (John 15:26-27; 16:7-11; Lk. 24:49; Acts 1:8).

(4) Did the Holy Spirit come upon the Apostles from the Father too?

Jesus received the Holy Spirit from the Father and sent Him to the Apostles (Acts 2:33); and through them and their successors, the Bishops, the same Spirit is given to all those who believe and are baptized (Acts 8:14-17).

(5) What will confirmation do for us?

The Holy Spirit which we receive in confirmation will make us:

(a) Active members of the Church.
(b) Alive in Jesus Christ as mature Christians.
(c) Able to do good just as Jesus Himself, having received the Holy Spirit, went about doing good (Acts 10:38).

(6) What are the fruits of the Holy Spirit?

The fruits of the Spirit are: Love, Joy, Peace, Patience, Kindness, Goodness, Faithfulness, Gentleness, Self Control (Gal. 5:22).

(7) What are the gifts of the Holy Spirit which come through the rite of confirmation?

The gifts are: Wisdom, understanding, knowledge, counsel, fortitude, piety and fear of the Lord (Is. 11:2).

(8) How do these wonderful seven gifts help you as Christians?

By the first four gifts – wisdom, understanding, knowledge, counsel – the Holy Spirit helps me to understand the truths of our holy religion. By the last three gifts – fortitude, piety and fear of the Lord – I am given the grace and power that my will needs to do what God wants me to do.

(9) For what purpose are the gifts given to us?

The gifts are given to us that we may use them to help one another to grow in Christ (1 Cor. 12:7).

(10) How is confirmation done?

(a) Each candidate goes to the Bishop. or
(b) The Bishop goes to each candidate.
(c) The candidate may give his own name as he comes forward or somebody else may call their names for the Bishop.
(d) The Bishop dips his right thumb in the Chrism (a holy oil) and makes the sign of the cross on the forehead of the one being confirmed, and says:

Olufemi or Emeka, BE SEALED WITH THE HOLY SPIRIT, THE GIFT OF THE FATHER.

The newly confirmed answers: Amen.

(11) Why does the Bishop lay hands on the one being confirmed? The Apostles performed the same action to pass on the Spirit of God to others (Acts 8:17; 19:6).

(12) Finally – Did God promise in the Old Testament that He will give us His Spirit?

Yes. Always remember Jeremiah 31:31-34; Is. 32:15; Ezekiel 11:19-20, Joel 2:28-29.

In all these passages, we hear our loving God telling us that a time will come when He will put His beautiful, loving, peaceful Spirit into us. When this happens, each person so given the Spirit will know God personally. Where the Spirit of God is, there you find PEACE, LOVE and POWER of God which will help you to live a very good Christian life.

(13) A good prayer to the Holy Spirit that you may wish to know:

Leader: Come Holy Spirit, fill the hearts of your faithful and kindle in them the fire of your love.

Leader: Send forth your Spirit and all the things shall be recreated.

All respond: And you shall renew the face of the earth.

Let us Pray:

O God, you instructed the hearts of the faithful by the light of the Holy Spirit. Guide us by your Spirit to desire only what is good and so always to find joy in His comfort. Through Christ our Lord. Amen.

See Question 27 for explanation of the Baptism in the Holy Spirit.

# Q. 57 Questions for you to answer

By his death and resurrection, Jesus conquered sin and death. Man is now saved. If this is true, and I believe it is true, why did Jesus still say that:

(a) One ought to be baptized? (Jn. 3:1-8).

(b) One ought to eat His body and drink His Blood to have life? (Jn. 6:51-58).

(c) One ought to receive the Holy Spirit? (Lk. 24:49).

(d) One ought to be forgiven by the Church? (Jn. 20:22).

(e) That the sick should be prayed over and anointed with *oil* in His Name? (James 5:13-16).

(f) Why is it that this should be done by those who have authority in the Church and not just anybody? (Acts 15:2-22f; 1 Tim. 5:17; Titus 1:5).

(g) Some people say that we are all priests (1 Pt. 2:9). If we are all priests, why is it that a human being is still to be "taken out among men and made their representative before God, to offer gifts and sacrifices for sins?" (Heb. 5:1-4). Why not everybody?

(h) Jesus, as God, can heal a sick person by uttering His Powerful Word, why did He resort to the use of mud and saliva in healing the blind man? (Jn. 9:6).

(i) Why was *oil* used as the medium through which miraculous healing was effected in Jesus Name? (Mk. 6:13).

(j) Why did the Bible attribute healing power to Moses fiery serpent? (Num. 21:8-9) or to the handkerchiefs which touched the body of Paul? (Acts 19:11-12).

(k) Some people say that the Holy Spirit is given directly to each person without an intermediary, say a Bishop's laying of hand. Why was it that God did not send the Holy Spirit directly on the seventy leaders but instead "took some of the Spirit he had given to Moses and gave it to the seventy leaders?" (Num. 11:24).

# Q. 58 What should be our attitude towards sinners?

**Pointless blaming sinners (Jn. 8:10-11; Lk. 7:36-48)**

"Woman ... has no one condemned you?"

"No one sir", she answered. Jesus said,

"Nor do I condemn you. You may go. But from now on, avoid this sin" (Jn. 8:10-11).

This passage of the scripture summarizes the attitude of Jesus towards sinners. He told us that He was sent to this world not to condemn sinners (Jn. 3:17). He came to save the world under the empire of sin. In His ministry, He never quarrelled with, ridiculed or laughed at sinners who were looking for forgiveness. Someone wrote in a magazine I have just finished reading: Jesus never said, 'I told you so'. In the story of the prodigal son, the common reaction of most parents would have been "Ah! You see yourself. Try it again and you will see pepper". Jesus told us in that parable that the father of the child immediately threw a party for the son who was regarded as dead and has now come back to life. Great God! Praise be to His Holy Name. The prophet Micah saw the whole point I am making here when he joyfully cried out to the Lord:

"What God can compare with you: taking fault away, pardoning crime, not cherishing anger for ever but delighting in showing mercy?" (Micah 7:18).

The Lord is so kind and considerate to us sinners. The Psalmist asks: If you O Lord kept a record of our sins, who could escape being condemned? (Ps. 130:3). Of course, no one. None of us is perfect, we are only forgiven.

This is not to say that Jesus loves sin or that it makes no difference to Him whether people sin or not. He did not give us license to sin because He has power to put our lives in order, no matter what we do. He knows the gravity of sin (Lk. 7:36-48) and on a few occasions in His ministry, He warned people not to sin again: To the man paralyzed for 38 years and who now had been healed, Jesus said: "Listen, you are well now; so stop sinning or something worse may happen to you" (Jn. 5:14); and to the woman accused to have been caught in the very act of adultery, Jesus said: "Woman, . . . has no one condemned you?" "No one sir", she answered, Jesus said, "Nor do I condemn you. You may go. But from now on, avoid this sin" (Jn. 8:10-11).

Jesus knows and has taught us by His own actions that there is no use blaming sinners or questioning them why and how they acted in the way they did. What is important when people are in sin, is that they are freed from their sin. People are not happy in sin, so they need freedom, not condemnation. The sinner requires mercy and help, not ridicule or quarrel. Is it not better to save a dying man than to quarrel and curse death? When Moses went to Pharaoh, all he asked Pharaoh was "Let my people go". Moses did not have to find out why the Israelites were in bondage or blame them for being there; he did not spend time weighing how far they had been faithful to God of Abraham. The people were in bondage. They were under pressure. All they needed was freedom. Perhaps, they sinned and that was why they were going through suffering but that was not the concern of Moses. He was not commissioned to set up an enquiry into the causes of their enslavement. We have a proverb in my town that "it is more reasonable to free a drowning man before you set up an enquiry into why he fell into the river". When you know a sinner, simply go to worry Jesus about the person's conversion.

The man paralyzed for 38 years had regained his freedom before Jesus issued him a warning: "Give up your sins so that something worse may not overtake you". That is a serious warning but it came at the appropriate time – a time when the man was disposed to listen. Previously, all such a warning would have been ineffective, for it wouldn't have made any difference in the man's condition. A great thinker (Aristotle) asks: What sermon can change an incontinent man – a man who has lost self-control?

This does not mean that people should be left in their morally dead condition or that they cannot change again. All one is saying is that we should look at sinners as human beings who need help, and charity demands that we help them to regain their liberty which Jesus has won for us by His obedient death on the cross.

The Pharisees ostracised sinners and condemned them. Jesus came to save sinners who wish to be saved. To ostracise or make fun of sinners is very much like avoiding or making fun of a person suffering from a disease of the sort that would be regarded as mentally defective.

As we look at people especially sinners, let us dwell, as the Bible teaches us, on the fine, good things in them. "Think about all you can praise God for and be glad about" in their lives (Phil. 4:8).

Before we sin, let us fear God's justice; if we however, fall into that misfortune of sinning, let us repent.

"Do not be so confident of pardon that you sin again and again. Do not say; 'His mercy is so great, he will pardon my sins, however many. To him belong both mercy and wrath ... Come back to the Lord without delay; do not put if off from one day to the next ..." (Eccl. 5:5).

## Blessed Assurance

The Bible teaches us that when we repent (sincerely make the decision to change our sinful life) and begin to live no longer for ourselves but for the glory of God, the Lord from then on accepts us, for that is His blessed will – that we repent and live. He does not wish the death of a sinner but that he REPENTS and live; only the living (those who are fully ALIVE) can praise the Lord.

# Q. 59 Why must we leave sin and bad company alone?

**We shall answer this question with a story:**
**The Story of Everyman who Faced Death**

We have been taught that we do not only avoid sin, we should avoid dangerous occasions of sin. We should not forget ourselves nor do we allow others to drag us into the mud. Recently, I read a story about Mr. Everyman. One day, he gave a dinner to his friends. In the midst of the dinner, the figure of Death appears and tells Everyman that his time on earth is up and he must go to the Judgment Seat of God. But Everyman whose life has left much to be desired, pleads with Death for just a few more days upon earth. Death refuses. Everyman pleads for just one more day. Again Death refuses. "Then give me just one hour", begs Everyman. So death consents to give him just sixty minutes during which time Everyman is to prepare himself for his ordeal at the Judgment Seat.

Then Death disappears. Everyman pleads with his friends at the dinner table to accompany him to the Judgment Seat of God, there to speak on his behalf. One by one they arise and leave the table. They have no particular wish to meet God as yet.

The next scene shows Everyman appealing to his relatives and finally to the woman with whom he has lived in sin. All refuse to accompany him to the Judgment Seat of God, there to testify on his behalf". (Cyprian Truss, *Say it with Stories* p. 48).

Sin, guilt, sorrow, death – all these rob us of the joy of salvation. But our God is merciful *and tender*. He will cause the bright dawn of salvation to rise upon us and to shine from heaven on all those who live in the dark shadow of death, to guide our steps into the path of peace (Lk. 1:78-79). If this will happen, we must heed the advice of Scripture:

"You must put to death, then, the earthly desires at work in you, such as sexual immorality, indecency, lust, evil passions, and greed (for greed is a form of idolatry). Because of such things; God's anger will come upon those who do not obey him. At one time you yourselves used to live according to such desires, when your life was dominated by them. But now you must get rid of all these things: *anger, passion and hateful feelings. No insults or obscene talk must ever come from your lips. Do not lie to one another, for you have taken off the old self with its habits and have put on the new self.* This is the new being which God, its Creator, is constantly renewing in his own image, in order to bring you to a full knowledge of himself" (Col. 3:5-10).

Do this and you will have the blessings of salvation which begins in this life – grace is the beginning of glory (Aquinas). In this life, there is joy in living with a clear conscience.

## Q. 60 Why does God allow us to be tested?

It remains true that God can neither deceive nor be deceived. As St. James says "God tempts no one" (James 1:13). Referring to the case of Ahab, God permitted him to be tested just as he permitted Satan to test the holy man, Job. The Lord said to Satan "All right, he is in your power, but you are not to kill him" (Job. 2:6).

Satan defeated Ahab but could not defeat Job. The curious question of course is: why did God permit the enemy to test them? In both cases, the character, virtues and the religious state of each person was revealed in their responses to their tests.

The story of Ahab is a warning to those who love lies. Ahab knew the truth. Prophet Micaiah warned him but Ahab preferred lies (1 Kings 22:1-40) to truth.

We have a lesson in the whole incident: A person is conquered by what he loves. If you prefer error and sin to truth, you will reap the fruit of error and sin. God teaches us this lesson in Ahab's disaster so that we do not go in the wrong direction.

## Q. 61 Do priests only have the best of Eucharistic Meal?

Some people believe that Priests are the only ones having the best of the "Eucharistic Meal" since they are privileged to take the consecrated Bread and Wine. A Catechism of Christian Doctrine which most of us studied holds that Christ is received whole and entire under either kind alone – Bread or Wine.

The understanding here is that the whole Christ is present, both in the Bread and in the Wine. So those who share in the Bread (the body) are sharing at the same time the Blood. Though while one receives our Lord in either way by itself, receiving under both forms more perfectly signifies our response to Jesus' command to eat his flesh and drink his blood, and our prayerful desire for the gift he promised to those who do so.

However, communion under both species was the standard practice up till 12th century as much theological and spiritual significance was placed on the sign value (Symbolism) of receiving the Lord in communion under the form of Bread and Wine. Even during this time, however, all the way back to the earliest years, Christians clearly understood that one did not have to receive both forms in order to truly receive the Lord. "Never was there some sort of gross supposition that in the Bread one received the dry Blood of Christ alone which later became alive with the Blood when one drank the Chalice (John J. Dietzen).

Communion under one kind, was therefore, not at all unusual from the beginning. The Eucharist would be taken to the sick at home under the form of Bread alone, no one doubted that the individual received the whole Sacrament. The sick who could not swallow the Bread were given communion only in the form of Wine.

Around 12th Century and at the birth of protestantism, some people in this rank started to push the idea that one did not receive the whole Christ if one only received either the Bread or the Wine. The Church to reject this error, stressed that Jesus was present whole and entire either in the Bread or in the Wine.

## Q. 62 What is Grace?

Some people think that 'Grace' is like liquid which God pours into the soul. Such an idea of Grace is not correct. Grace (Karis, Gratia-Greek, Latin) in theology means precisely God self-communication; God-coming-down-to-dwell-in-me. Grace means God making Himself as a Gift to me. For us in a precise way, it means eternal life through Jesus Christ. The law was given to the old testament people, but through Jesus Christ, we have "received grace upon grace", that is, God in Christ, has poured the fullness of His love into our hearts (Romans 5:5; 6:23; John 1:16-17).

Grace (God-who-dwells-in-me-now) is God's gift to us NOW. Because we are graced (God has decorated and elevated us beyond our natural condition), we are therefore able to know and love God without yet seeing Him face to face. Because we are graced, we are able to live well, live the right sort of life Jesus lived.

When people are not able to live the life of charity, if they are not able to be humble, chaste, but rather follow the demands of their flesh, the basic reason is that either they have thrown their gift away or they have not allowed this grace to operate in their life. To live well and attain everlasting happiness, one must be deeply united with the Lord Jesus because cut away from him, we perish (John 15:1-6). So you can call Jesus 'God's grace to the world'.

## Q. 63 Does the Bible teach that Man evolved from matter?

We have heard so much about Darwinian theory of evolution which tries to show that man evolved from matter; thus the idea of man in the garden of Eden (Adam and Eve) who originated from God, as the Bible teaches, seems to make no sense. We do not want to contend with Darwinian theory, but it might be necessary to say that we do not hold the view of Darwin for the simple reason that it does not tell us the origin of Substance (aggregation of substances). It should be noted that the problem of the origin of man is closely tied up with the problem of the origin of the Universe. It is not enough to say that the Universe originated from "One Gigantic Egg" as I heard from VOA one day. We would want to know the origin of the big "egg" of which man is a part. The separation of primitive or scientific anthropology and cosmology confuses the issue the more.

However, the assertion that God made man, which is our thesis and belief, needs to be clarified. According to the Bible, matter originated from God (if matter were not eternal, it will need to be shown how it came about) and so the theological understanding of "Creatio ex Nihilo" (Creation from nothing) does not apply to man – man, as the Bible teaches, was fashioned from what is already in existence – dust of the earth.

I do not see any problem in saying that man developed (or evolved) but I cannot subscribe to the idea that man is what he is by the power of evolution, for that would make evolution a god. It is our belief that God is the Creator of man and of all that there is.

I stated earlier that man's origin should not be separated from the origin of the Universe because if we are to account for how a given system is and functions, we should be able to offer a similar account for its parts. If the Universe cannot account for itself and is therefore caused, then man, who cannot originate himself (for to originate oneself, one has to exist prior to oneself, which is impossible) is the work of an intelligence (God).

Scripture does not tell us that man's appearance is a 'mediate' action of an agent (angel, demiurge, or evolution etc). But assuming that man's origin is a result of a 'mediate' action, it does not disprove the Bible's view that man is the work of God. Each person now in existence is the result of corporate action of two persons but it does not mean that God has no hand in each person's appearance on earth. The law of how things should come to be is the work of God, hence man, no matter how he came about, is the work of God.

# Q. 64 What counts in the eyes of God?

In terms of value, what does the Bible say is God's priority consideration? I wish to point them out here to put order into our prayer life (Lk. 11:9-13).

## (1) The Holy Spirit

"The Lord says, "The time is coming when I will make a new covenant with the people of Israel and with the people of Judah. It will not be like the old covenant that I made with their ancestors when I took them by the hand and led them out of Egypt. Although I was like a husband to them, they did not keep that covenant. The new covenant that I will make with the people of Israel will be this: I will put my law within them and write it on their hearts. I will be their God, and they will be my people. None of them will have to teach his fellow countryman to know the LORD, because all will know me, from the least to the greatest. I will forgive their sins and I will no longer remember their wrongs. I, the LORD, have spoken" (Jeremiah 31:31-34).

"And I myself will send upon you what my Father has promised. But you must wait in the city until the power from above comes down upon you" (Luke 24:49).

"There are different kinds of Spiritual gifts, but the same Spirit gives them. There are different ways of serving but the same Lord is served. There are different abilities to perform service, but the same God gives ability to everyone for their particular service. The Spirit's presence is shown in some way in each person for the good of all. The Spirit gives one person a message full of wisdom, while to another person the same Spirit gives a message full of knowledge. One and the same Spirit gives faith to one person, while to another person he gives the power to heal. The Spirit gives one person the power to work miracles; to another, the gift of speaking God's message; and to yet another, the ability to tell the difference between gifts that come from the Spirit and those that do not. To one person he gives the ability to speak in strange tongues, and to another he gives the ability to explain what is said. But it is one and the same Spirit who does all this as he wishes, he gives a different gift to each person" (Corinthians 12:4-11).

(2) **Reconciliation - (Eph. 4:17-32)**

"It is true, of course, that "all of us have knowledge", as they say.

Such knowledge, however, puffs a person up with pride; but love builds up. Whoever thinks he knows something really doesn't know as he ought to know. But the person who loves God is known by him" (1 Corinthians 8:1-3).

"Whoever thinks he is standing firm had better be careful that he does not fall. Every test that you have experienced is the kind that normally comes to people. But God keeps his promise, and he will not allow you to be tested beyond your power to remain firm; at the time you are put to the test, he will give you the strength to endure it, and so provide you with a way out" (1 Corinthians 10:12-13).

(3) **Humility**

"But the grace that God gives is even stronger. As the Scripture says, "God resists the proud, but gives grace to the humble" (James 4:6).

"Humble yourselves, then, under God's mighty hand, so that he will lift you up in his own good time. Leave all your worries with him, because he cares for you" ( 1 Peter 5:5-7).

(4) **Wisdom**

"God gave Solomon unusual wisdom and insight, and knowledge too great to be measured. Solomon was wiser than the wise men of the East or the wise men of Egypt. He was the wisest of all men: wiser than Ethan the Ezrahite, and Heman, Calcol and Darda, the sons of Mahol, and his fame spread throughout all the neighboring countries. He composed three thousand proverbs and more than a thousand songs. He spoke of trees and plants, from the Lebanon cedars to the hyssop that grows on walls; he talked about animals, birds, reptiles, and fish. Kings all over the world heard of his wisdom and sent people to listen to him" (1 Kings 4:29-34).

(5) **Knowledge of the Mysteries of the Kingdom**

"At that time Jesus was filled with joy by the Holy Spirit and said, "Father; Lord of heaven and earth! I thank you because you have shown to the unlearned what you have hidden from the wise and learned. Yes, Father; this was how you were pleased to have it happen. My Father has given me all things. No one knows who the Son is except the Father; and no one knows who the Father is except the Son and those to whom the Son chooses to reveal him" (Luke 10:21-22).

# Q. 65    When is war morally right?

(1) The question is often asked by moralists and religious people whether a war is morally right and justifiable. It can be argued that the goal of any war is the establishment of peace; therefore a war, though in itself an evil, can be prosecuted in the pursuit of peace. The argument against this view is that a good end in view cannot justify the use of an evil means to achieve such an end.

(2) Some Moralists argue that a war can be waged against an aggressor if:

    [a] Every possible avenue of peace had been explored and used without any success.

    [b] The effects of such a war (the destructions that will result from it) should not exceed the injustice to be set right. The war then should be limited.

(3) As can be seen, the problem with determining the effect of a war that can be said to be corrective in proportion to the injustice it is meant to correct, is indeed very difficult. Only an infinite mind can assess and mete out justice as would be proportionate to injustice committed.

(4) For example, if a war is to be waged to punish country X for invading country Y, damage to be inflicted on country X must be in proportion to the damage which she caused country Y. But I do not think that it is possible for anyone to repair an injustice which has been done to something or some person or persons.

(5) While war (brute force) is not an intelligent solution to injustice, an appeasement of an oppressor/aggressor is morally wrong.

## Q. 66   Why is it always difficult to describe one's experience of God or the spiritual world?

Most mystics do not bother to describe their experiences of God or Spiritual World because they fear that they might not be able to give a satisfactory account of what they know. One can understand their problem: If I have an experience of an unfamiliar coloured object in one act of intuition (a flash of insight) as I reflect on the world around me, it would be impossible for me to talk about this coloured object using our colour language.

The best I can do is to compare it with coloured objects of our experiences. I might also warn that the comparison is odious for it does not really give the true picture. This is the logical difficulty in the mystic's way of speaking. But some critical thinkers have argued that if the mystic admits that "the object of his vision is something which cannot be described, then he is bound to talk nonsense when he describes it" (A.J. Ayer, Language Truth and Logic, p. 124). I do not think that Ayer's conclusion is correct. A person who says: "I cannot describe X" and on second thought attempts to do so, may not necessarily end up talking nonsense. She might be able to provide some kind of descriptions of her experience which may not give us the exact picture of what she experienced but may give us some clues as to the nature of the sort of thing she is talking about.

There are other problems which may inhibit a reliable account of the mystic's experience. These may also include actions of interfering spirits. Most mystics do say that such spirits exist and that they are serious menaces to the life of the mystic. We dare not discuss this problem since its consideration would be proper in the treatise on the methods of discernment of spiritual entities in religion.

W. T. Stace thinks that mystic's reticence may also be that "they fear ridicule or at least a callous and unsympathetic reception" (Stace, Mysticism and Philosophy, p. 58). The attitude of the mystic in general is silence over what is experienced for it would be improper to throw a piece of gold to a dog.

There are people who do not only ridicule the Mystic, but think that it will damage their own intellectual reputation or that it will be an admission of mental laziness or lack of intellectual maturity to believe the mystic.

Whoever holds such a view is mistaken. In addition, the argument that what the mystic claims to know is not true, either because one does not know it or that such claims seem strange to believe, is very weak. We may never find out personally what the mystic claims to know. All that is needed is that we carefully ask her the right questions and check her claims vis-a-vis already known cases and to see if the evidences of her claims are strong.

It is also pointless to argue that because the experience of the mystic is very "private" (Bertrand Russell), one cannot ascribe validity to such claims. One who holds such a view, if he is to be taken seriously, should be prepared to say that for purpose of knowing the truth, one should never believe anything until one has a personal knowledge of such a thing. H. D. Lewis gives a better attitude here:

"When therefore a claim is made to have a direct experience of God we cannot rule this out just because we do not have this experience ourselves and can form little conception of what it would be like. If we did so we would, moreover, be putting ourselves in a odd position vis-a-vis those who say they have no sort of religious awareness. But there could be other reasons for disallowing the claim" (H. D. Lewis, Philosophy of Religion, p. 203).

## Q. 67    Who are the holy souls?

(1) In his anguish, the holy man, Job recalls the pitiable aspect of the human person:
"Remember that you made me from clay" (Job 10:9). Job's statement is only to show that the human person is a very frail (weak and fragile) being but in Gn. 2:7 the reality of the human history is stated: "You were made from soil, and you will become soil again" (Gn. 3:19). This statement could lead someone to the conclusion that there can be no life after death. But the Bible also comforts the living; the souls of the just are at peace: "they have the confident hope of immortality. Their sufferings were minor compared with the blessings they will receive" (Wisdom 3:1-9). In God's plan therefore, there is no death and annihilation (of Wisdom 2:23; 1 Cor. 15:12-58; try to reflect on verse 29). Beyond the grave, life continues. This is the teaching of the Bible and the Holy Catholic Church and Catholic mystics. The possibility of such a life lies in the omnipotent power of the risen and ever-living Jesus, God-made-man. In other words, the possibility of surviving out bodily disintegrations rests on the power of God who brought Jesus into the everlasting age through His death on the cross. It is because JESUS has conquered death that we too hope to live in another life in a way impossible to explain.

Those who have died and one yet not in the presence of God but hope to be ultimately with God are called "Holy Souls".

We examine here the Bible teaching and the Church's view on the **Holy Souls.**

**The Bible passages to be consulted are:**
(1) 2 Maccabees 12:38-45. The Bible stipulates here what should be done for those souls who were killed in battle.

(2) Tobit 4:17. This is Tobit's advice to Tobias: At the death of God's faithful, Tobias was advised to prepare food and put it on the grave. The curious question is: For what reason was this done? We shall examine the intent of the practice.

(3) 1 Cor 15:12-58; Wisdom Ch. 3 take up a discussion on the souls of the dead – they are still alive and Mk. 12:18-27 makes it a matter of logic: if God addressed Himself to Moses as the God of Abraham, Isaac, and Jacob, the Hebrew patriarchs who were already dead, then for God, these Patriarchs were alive, for God could not have called Himself their God if they were dead (completely dissolved into the soil in which they were buried). God cannot and is not God for what is dead. The logic is this: God sees the "dead" as alive. He couldn't see them as alive unless they were truly so. On this argument, see my book, A Theological Enquiry into Questions People Ask, Q60. There is a new book on this subject of Holy Souls by Fr. Allessio Parente O. F. M. Cap: THE HOLY SOULS?, published by Our Lady of Grace, Capuchin Friary, Foggia, Italy, 1988.

Having introduced the subject matter, let us do a detailed study of the state of the souls who are not on earth or in heaven. Are they in hell? Some people say that after death, it is either "Heaven or Hell". The Catholic Church says that it is not always heaven or hell; there is another state, PURGATORY. The word "Purgatory" is derived from "Purgare" which means "to purge", "to cleanse". The word "purus" is pure and "agere" is "to make", "to do".

If you join "purus" to "agere", you will get the meaning: "to make pure". So "Purgare" (purgation) is a state after death wherein the soul finally renounces Self-love and accepts God's love fully. The instance of this acceptance of God's love is the end of purgation and the beginning of glory.

(From Allessio Parente O. F. M. Cap: The Holy Souls) "The dying Tobias said to his son: 'Place your bread on the tomb of the righteous, and gather the poor around it to eat and drink'" (Tob 4:17). This was because he believed that any act of charity done for the poor had a purifying effect which benefited departed souls.

In the book of Maccabees, it is reported that after the battle against Gorgias' men, Judas "made a collection and sent it to Jerusalem so that a sin offering could be for the souls of those who had died in battle, as it was holy and beneficial to pray for the dead, so that they could have been freed from their sin...He made atonement for the dead that they might be delivered from their sin" (2 Macc. 12:45).

In chapter 12 of Saint Matthew's Gospel, Jesus speaks about sins against the Holy Spirit which cannot be pardoned even in the other world (Mt. 12:32). As a consequence of this statement, then, there must be a place in the other world where sins can be remitted. In chapter 5 of the same Gospel, Jesus warns us to make peace with our enemies: "Make friends quickly with your accuser while there is still time" (Mt. 5:25). Otherwise at the end of our lives he will put us into the hands of the Judge who will send us to a jail from which we will not be freed until we have paid all our debts. According to the teaching of Jesus, our enemy is the devil or our conscience. If we don't do penance for our sins in the present life, they will be our accusers before the Judge, the Lord, who will put us into the hands of his ministers, the angels, and they will bring us to the expiation place of Purgatory, which we will not leave until all our sins are expiated.

## Q. 68 Does anybody have power to forgive sin?

**Answer:**

(1) The Bible says that "God is the only one who can forgive sins" (Mk 2:9, Acts 10:40-45). Equally too only God has power to drive out demons, heal and raise the dead. God can do all these because only He has the power to give life and conquer death and the devil.

(2) But the Bible says that God can give human beings power to do some of what He Himself does:
"Believers will be given the power to perform miracles......" (Mk 16:17; 1 Cor 11:10);
"Receive the Holy Spirit, if you forgive people's sins, they are forgiven......."(Jn 20:22).

(3) It is clear from the passages of the Bible referred to here that some works which only God can do, can also be done by a human being if God gives him the power to do so. What becomes clear then is that a person can only perform such actions in the name of God; it is God who gives such power to people.

(4) We read in the Bible then that it is not everyone in the church who has the power to heal, work miracles, discern the spirit or to forgive sins. God has arranged these ministries so that they can be carried out in an orderly manner (1 Cor. 11:27-30; 13:40) in His Church.

(5) We also read in the Bible that the power to forgive sins was specifically given to the Apostles (Jn. 20:22). Neither Mark 16:17 nor 1 Cor 11:4-11 which mentions the gifts which the believer can receive and exercise, mentions the power to forgive people's sins as a gift which anybody can receive and exercise. According to St. John (Jn 20:22), Jesus gave the power to forgive sins to the Apostles. W. Lock, an Anglican Bible Scholar (it is good to hear what a non-Catholic thinks about this passage of the Bible) says:

"The gift is not here the power of deciding between right and wrong actions, as in Mt. 18:18 ('whatever things....') but of dealing with persons, 'whosoever sins' (in Acts 2:41, 5:1-11, 13:10-12; 1 Cor 5:4; 2 Cor 2:6); their decision is treated as at once ratified in heaven (in Jn 16:23);....."

("The Gospel According to St. John" in A New Commentary on Holy Scripture including the Apocrypha, edited by Charles Gore and other, London: 1928)

(6) In the Church then, there are certain powers which are vested only in specific offices. For example, it is the episkopos (the Bishop) who has the power to ordain a priest. In the early Church, there were different classes of ministers (Eph. 4:11) with specific powers:

[1]    Presbyters (Elders 1 Tm. 5:17-25)
[2]    Episkopos (Bishop 1 Tm 3:1-7)
[3]    Deacons (1 Tim 3:8-13)
(Read Q.43 4-7 of this book).

All these offices have their specific powers for services in the Church. So, while varieties of gift can be exercised by the priestly faithful (1 Cor 12:4-11, 1 Pt. 1:9), the power to forgive sin is in the office of the ordained minister.

## Q. 69  Is it superstitious to wear blessed medals, finger rosaries, crucifixes, bones of saints, scapulars, etc?

**Answer:**

(1) In the Catholic Church teaching, blessed objects (medals, crucifixes, bones of the saints, etc.) are called sacramentals. Like pictures of things, they help to remind us of what they stand for and our minds are set on God while having them. Through their use, God offers His children the help they so much need. An example in the Bible is this:

"Elisha died and was buried". A dead body was thrown into his tomb. "As soon as the body touched Elisha's bones, the man came back to life and stood up" (2 Kings 13:20-21).

# Prolog

After going through this collection of scriptural passages which has been used to explain some of the Catholic beliefs and practices, I hope that you will now be in the position to understand some of the things you see the Catholic Church do. In addition, I hope also that you would have benefited from reading through the scriptural passages cited.

May the Blessed Virgin, Mother of the Church, assist us in our desire to know her Son, Amen.

# TOPICAL INDEX

# Other Books by Fr. Jude

## On the Eucharist, a Divine Appeal

This book, edited by Fr. Jude, recounts a series of revelations from the Lord to a young religious, Sr. Anna Ali. Jesus appears to Sr. Anna, a victim soul, to give her messages of His Love, Mercy, and Justice. He explains why He is appearing at this time in history, focusing on His great Love and Mercy, shown to us by His Presence in the Holy Eucharist. The messages tell of our Lord's loneliness and sorrow because so many of us have abandoned Him, and how He yearns for our return. This book renews the true Presence of Jesus Christ in the Holy Eucharist in the heart and soul of the reader. $11.95 plus S&H.

## Power in the Bread

Plunge into the mystery of the Holy Eucharist with this book by Fr. Jude. Drawing upon Scripture, and the Holy Fathers and Doctors of the Church, Fr. Jude writes so that all can grow in this great mystery which "is not something magical; it is mystical". Learn what Scripture says about the Eucharist; the love with which Jesus wants to transform us in this Sacrament; how we should prepare for this greatest of all graces. These meditations bring the reader to a deeper appreciation of the Mystery at the Heart of our Faith. $7.95 plus S&H.

## Beyond Words

The definitive examination of mystical experience. What is mysticism? Is the mystical state possible? Do all mystical experiences come from God? Fr. Jude answers these questions and more, assuring us that mysticism is not only possible, but the destiny of every person. $9.95 plus S&H.

## Distributed by: